I'MNOT BROKEN

Surviving the House of Demons

JESSICA L REALE

To those who have stuck by me even when I made it very difficult.

Tami, your dedication to me has never wavered. I will be forever grateful that you chose to stick around. Thank you for showing me how a Mom should love.

Rob, thank you for being my rock and helping me create and care for our family.

Alexia, your memory will always live on. I hope I have made you proud. My favorite memory of you is that you always would pick the Gardenia's by the front door. Keep picking those flowers, my Angel.

Chapter I

"Granny, why are we moving again?" I asked. Well, your mommy is going to have a baby, and we are moving to be near them and her soon-to-be husband. Oh, so we will finally live together as a family? No response. We move to a motel across the street from the Santa Cruz Beach Boardwalk. I am fascinated with all the lights and sounds coming from the boardwalk. Hopefully, mommy will take me on the rides if I am a good girl. I start a new school. I am in the first grade. Kids make fun of me for living in the motel. Being teased makes me sad. We do not live in a motel room. Granny and I live in the attached two-bedroom apartment because my Granny works at the motel's front desk. That is how it always is, just Granny and me. She always takes care of me when my mom decides to go on another adventure. I miss mommy, but when she is around, she always is annoyed with me, and it makes me upset. I am happier when she leaves us alone.

I finish the first grade with a lot of help. Reading was hard for me. I am glad the school year is over. I have a best friend named Haley. She lives down the street with her mom in an apartment. I love having sleepovers at her house. Haley's mom takes us to fun places and plays games with us. She is silly and fun. I wish my mom was like Haley's mom. My mom does not seem to like me much. Haley and I spend a lot of time together over the summer, playing and swimming in the motel pool. I swim so much that my blonde hair turns green from the chlorine in the pool. Granny is not too happy about the fact that we have to get a special shampoo to get the green out. I even got to go to the boardwalk a couple of times with Granny, Haley, and her mom. Best summer ever.

The summer of 1990 ends. It is time to start the second grade. I like my teacher. His name is Mr. Berryman-Shafer. He is fun. If we get the answers to questions correct, he will throw peanuts at us. I am doing much better in school this year. Haley is also in my class. We get to sit next to each other. I still do not see my mom much, but I meet her boyfriend, Charles, and his three daughters. Each time I see my mom, her stomach is so much bigger. She told me it is my new baby brother growing in there.

On October 8, 1990, my brother Chad was born. He is cute and so tiny. A few weeks later, my mom visits the motel to see us. She brings Chad over. My Granny says she is in baby heaven, cuddled up with him. I am not happy. That is my Granny. I do not want to share her. I want my mom to go home and take Chad with her. To my surprise, my mom does leave but does not take Chad. Granny says he is going to live with us now. I do not want Chad to stay with us because babies are loud. I do not want to share a room. I am lucky Chad does not share my room. Chad sleeps in a crib in Granny's room and takes up a lot of her time.

The new year comes, and my mom is getting married to Charles. I am so excited to be a part of the wedding. My stepsister Diana is just a little older than me. We are in matching black and gold velvet dresses, and we walk behind my mom to carry the train of her dress. Chad is wearing a baby-sized suit. My Granny told me that my mom getting married will be great for the family and we will all live together soon. I hope so because I miss my mom when she is not around. My mom looks so beautiful in her white dress. I hope the wedding means getting to be with my mom more. I was wrong. She chose Charles and his girls over us. Over the next year, I do not see her much.

Another summer ends. The third grade starts, and the three of us still live in the motel. Chad is now almost one and trying to walk. Man, does he get into so much stuff. My mom is pregnant again. On September 23, 1991, my little sister was born. It is not long before my newborn sister Alexia lives with Granny, Chad, and me. I do not understand how my mom keeps having babies and gives them to my Granny. Chad begins sleeping in Granny's bed so Alexia can have his crib. Nothing changes. I keep going to school while I try to help Granny with the babies since she is still running the motel front desk. My mom lives with Charles and his daughters, not seeing us much.

In early 1992 Granny, my mom, Charles, Chad, Alexia, and I moved to Stagecoach, Nevada as a family. Charles's three daughters do not move with us. They are living with their mom in California. I am nervous about starting a new school. However, I am happy to be living full-time with my mom again. My mom and stepfather Charles bought a double-wide mobile home on five acres. This is the nicest home I have ever lived in. I have my own room, which I love because my two siblings are still babies and get into all my things. My Granny has her own room. Chad and Alexia share a room.

My mom is pregnant again. I thought things would be better living as a family, you know, with a mom and dad, but I was wrong. Everything is the same. I only really see my mom if she is yelling at me or having me take care of the babies or our dogs. My mom had her fourth baby in August 1992. Michael only lived with us for a few weeks until the doctor said he could fly. My mom left and took him to Pennsylvania, where she gave him up for adoption to an old family friend.

School is going well, and I am making friends. Charles stays in his office most of the time. I rarely have any interaction with him. Granny takes care of the home and all of us kids. When my mom comes out of her room, she mainly checks on the English Bulldogs she breeds for income. I have noticed my mom is being mean to Alexia often. If Alexia does cry, my mom does not tend to her and will just leave her for someone else to take care of. She even offered to give Alexia away to a woman who owned a horse my mom was looking to buy. Another time I saw her run a lit lighter under Alexia's bare feet as she sat in the highchair. I never said anything about it because, honestly, she scares me. One time, she chased me around the yard with a fly swatter because I accidentally sprayed her with a hose while she was sunbathing. Things are not going well in her marriage; before I know it, we are moving again.

Another town, another new school. The new house we are renting is not as nice or as big as our other house. I will not be getting my own room this time. It is a two-bedroom mobile home in a cul-de-sac. My mom has taken the master bedroom, so Granny, Chad, Alexia, and I have to share one room. My Granny and Chad share a full-size bed in the room. Alexia and I have bunk beds. There is little space to move around, but we make it work. The neighbors are friendly, and they have kids my age that I play with. I spend my summer with the neighbor's son playing make-believe, digging in the dirt, and laughing. The mountains are out in the backyard, and there are ditches I ride my bike in. The school year starts, and I am in the fifth grade. New schools mean new friends. I find making friends hard for me. I never know how long I will be living in a town.

My mom is not around much, and when she is, my mom is unpredictable. My mom changes a lot during the time she is away. My mom is very skinny, has scabs on her face, and is always shaky. I think when she moves all the time, she must have ants in her pants. We are okay because my

Granny takes care of us. My Granny makes having limited funds and no car work. Granny takes care of everything. She takes us to the doctor, feeds us, and makes sure I have school supplies. I have to have a cyst removed from my tailbone. My Granny took me to the hospital to have my surgery. Then she had to pay for the cab that took us home after the surgery. My mom could not be bothered to come home so we could use the car. My mom always says she is working, but we never see any benefits from it. Even with her being gone 90% of the time, she will not let me use the master bedroom. The more my mom is away, the more I want to be with her. I would do anything to have her pay attention to me.

The summer before sixth grade and my mom comes home for a visit. I latch on. My mom asked me to go with her on a trip. I am so excited to be with her. I do not care what we will be doing. The road trip to California was long.

We sleep in the car. On the way, we only get the stuff to make sandwiches and keep moving. It is just her and I, and I am so happy. Nothing could bring me down. We have little money, so our sandwiches are bread with ketchup. We listen to music laughing and talking. I want my mom to always be around. We made it to the Bay Area and finally got a hotel room. I am excited about a shower and bed. It is an adventure with my mom. My mom even takes me swimming in the hotel pool, we have no swim suites, but it does not matter. All that matters to me is we are having a blast diving and splashing. I do not want to go back to the hotel room.

Back in the room, things change, and Charles is there. I am confused as to why he would be there since they are not married anymore. In an instant, my mom changes. She is no longer fun and loving. She gives me money and tells me to walk across the four-lane highway to the grocery store to buy a cake mix. It is night and dark, but I go. I want to make her happy. I got back to the hotel room, and she makes the spice cake in the rice cooker. Once done, I have a slice. My mom then settles me into bed. I am not even asleep when she leaves me alone with Charles. I ask him where she went, and he just said she needs to get something.

I nod and try to go to sleep. Charles climbs into the bed next to me. I stiffen and hold the blankets tight up to my chin. He reaches over and starts rubbing my breasts. I ask him to stop, but he goes on, inching closer to my back, still rubbing on me; he tells me that touching them will help them grow. I say nothing. I try to become as small as possible and wish for my mom to come back. Charles keeps touching me, moving lower toward my privates. I finally get up, taking the blanket with me. I go close myself in the hotel closet. Knowing he can still get to me but hoping he will not. Thankfully, he leaves me alone. This is the last trip I will willingly take with my mother. I instead choose to stay home with Granny, where I am safe.

It is midsummer, and once again, we are moving. I really want to stay in Cold Springs, I have friends here, and I finally feel accomplished in school. I hate packing up another house and leaving behind things and memories. My mom makes me travel with her to our new rental home in Rancho Cordova, California. She says it is because she needs my help moving into the new house. I am just barely 11 years old. How much help does she think I will be? Either way, I have no choice. Good girls listen and do as they are told. My mom is changing; she looks too skinny and is never happy. If I listen, hopefully, she will be happy. Charles shows up on the trip back to NV to get the rest of our stuff. I am at once on edge. Mom says we need his larger van to get the last of our belongings, and he offers to help. I say nothing and get in the back of the van and buckle up. The drive is long, and we do not get back to NV until the early morning hours. Mom decides we should sleep in the van, so we do not wake up Granny and my siblings.

I lay down on the long seat in the back of the van and curl up with a blanket. My mom is sleeping on a chair further back in the van next to Charles. I wake up just as the sun is starting to rise. I wish it were the sunlight or the temperature in the van that woke me up, but sadly it is not. Charles is kneeling beside me, leaning over me to touch my breasts.

I keep rolling and moving away, but all I am doing is getting closer to the van wall. I do not know what to do. My mom is back there. I hear her moving about and talking nonsense. She is not helping me. I do not know how long she lets him touch me. In my mind, it is hours, but I am sure it was only minutes. My mom finally takes some action and yells at Charles. She whacks him on the head with some pole that was in the van. She tells him to stop touching me, and he does while rubbing his head. She says nothing to me. She stares at me, looking angry. I did nothing wrong. I figure it is late enough to go into the house, and I really need to pee anyway. I take off out of the van and run into the house to my Granny. I feel safe again. My Granny asks me why I am upset I say nothing. It does not do any good to share anyway. The ride back to the new house is a quiet one for me. We are all in the van making the long trip across the state. I talk to Granny some and keep my siblings entertained. When we make it to the new house, I am relieved that Charles does not stick around.

This summer is the same. I am trying to make new friends before I start sixth grade. It is hard being at another new house and school. This year Chad begins kindergarten. He is so excited. I wish I felt the same. My mom is never around, and when she comes home, she is so scary looking, with wild eyes all sunken in. She is too skinny. She hides in her room when she is home, only coming out to yell at us kids for playing too loudly. I am growing up, and no one will talk to me about the changes in my body. My Granny just brushes me off, and my mom walks right out the door any time I get to talk to her. I am eleven and have horrible stomach pains; my insides want to fall out. No one helps me. Granny is busy with the little kids. Finally, I figure out the issue myself; I got my period. I tell my mom, and she tosses' two pads at me and asks me if that is enough until she gets back. I tell her I have no idea because I do not. She leaves the house and returns late at night, but at least she remembers the pads. I want to ask her questions like can I shower? What can I take for the pain? But she leaves again. I cry myself to sleep, letting the warmness of the waterbed soothe my cramps.

The summer continues with much of the same. Me trying to make friends with the neighborhood kids while getting ready for school. My mom comes around once a month or so, on the first of the month, when the food stamps are received. This allows my Granny to use the car to get groceries for the month. Chad and I make some friends. They like to play make-believe in the backyard shed and play with our dogs. My brother Chad gets his leg stuck in the cracked plastic of the empty outdoor hot tub. My Granny freaks out and calls the police. The fire department comes out and was able to get him unstuck. He is laughing and having a great time, not worried at all. The coolest part about that day is we were allowed to explore the fire truck.

Us kids are not allowed in my mom's room even though she is really never home. Chad and I like to play in there. Alexia is still too little and does not play with us that often. Mostly she is my Granny's baby and is with her most of the time. We have English bulldogs that my mom breeds to sell and make money. They are expensive show dogs with papers and everything. There is one puppy left, and he is a runt. She was having trouble selling him. I asked if he could be my dog because I took care of him and played with him so much. I name him Snow because he is all white. That puppy is my best friend. I take care of him well. School starts in a couple of weeks, and my mom is due home to get us food, school clothes, and supplies.

Chad and I are playing in her room and getting into her things. We want to play hide and seek, so we want access to the closet. We move bags and clothes. Then Chad finds this hard black/brown ball of hard goop in a small plastic bag. We flush it down the toilet. I thought it was drugs, but I was not sure. Granny had said she thought my mom was doing drugs because of how she is changing, and to just try to stay out of her way. My mom could not find the drugs we flushed. My mom is angry and yelling about having to give the drugs to someone or pay the money for them, which is expensive. Chad and I are in the kitchen by the island getting yelled at, and she wants to know where it is. Chad is just four at the time, scared and crying so much. He does not think to lie, and he says he flushed it. In a second, her arm cocks back, and she punches him in the face so hard he falls back and hits his head on the sliding glass door. I do not move a muscle, too scared of what she would do next. Granny hears the commotion and yells at my mom that we are just kids and to stop. My mom is not listening, but eventually, she got her things and left. From then on, Chad and I stay out of her room and away from her things.

I keep caring for my puppy, Snow, long daily walks, and all. If I did not have a waterbed, I would have had him sleep in my bed with me. Chad's face heals up quickly, thankfully, because we are starting school. School starts the sixth grade for me and kindergarten for Chad. The school is just down the street and can easily be seen from our house. Granny lets us walk without her to school. I love walking with Chad. He is so cute with his backpack, which seems too big for his body. He walks ahead with his hands on his hips, calling for me to hurry up. Things are always best when my mom is not around. A couple of months later, things are good, and I really enjoy my art class. Chad turns five that October, and Alexia turned four that September. My mom starts coming home more often, all happy. She says she is dating someone, and she is thrilled. But her happiness never lasts long with us. One evening I am watching TV with Granny and Chad in the living room after dinner.

My mom was actually being a mom that evening and got the bath water ready for Alexia. Alexia is placed in the tub, and she starts screaming hot, over and over. My mom yells at her to shut up. She washes her harshly and makes her stay in the too-hot water. Alexia cries in Granny's arms for a long time that night. Her bottom and the back of her legs are all red. I feel so bad for her, but none of us could stop my mom.

Granny jokes that she wishes I did not have to go to school or that I could take Snow with me because he cries in his crate, waiting for me to come home. I love that puppy and feel proud knowing I take good care of him. The drugs have changed my mom, she was never very loving, but she would at least acknowledge us and allow us to be with her before. One day I come home from school, and Snow is gone. I ask my mom where my dog was, and she laughs at me and says it is my dog, so I sold him. I need the money. She promised me she would not sell him; I have never cried so hard before that day. I also learn never to anger her because she will find any way to hurt me. A few weeks later, she comes home for her monthly visit but tells us that she married a man named Larry and that we would be moving to his home in Elk Grove. I am upset because I do not want to go to another school in the middle of the school year. We know we do not have a choice but to move. Granny wants to stay at least until the summer. My mom yells at Granny that we are her kids, and she is taking us with her when she moves. Mom tells Granny if you do not like it, get your own place. It is always funny to me that we are her kids when she wants something from us or when she wants control; any other time, she is content to allow Granny to take care of us.

Chapter 2

We meet and move in with Larry all in one day. He seems like a nice man; his house is nice, with a basketball hoop and a hot tub in the backyard. It is only a 3-bedroom house, so it is a tight fit for us all. My mom has the master bedroom with Larry. I get my own room, and Granny shares her room with Chad and Alexia. I start another school to finish my sixth-grade year. It is challenging starting school again. I hate going. I have no friends, and a couple of boys often pick on me. I find it odd that my mom does not put Chad in Kindergarten again. She just says it is not a law, and she keeps him home. Chad wants to go to school and play with friends. My mom decides to send Chad away. My

Granny tries to talk her out of it but eventually agrees it would be better for him in a new home. We take Chad to the Sacramento Airport and send him all the way to Pennsylvania. He is sent to live with my youngest brother Michael. The man who adopted Michael wants to adopt Chad too. I miss Chad, but it is better for him. Mom is getting crazier by the day. School is hard, and I miss too many days. I must stay at the after-school session for the rest of the year to keep myself from repeating the sixth grade. It makes for a long day since it is an extra hour of school, but at least I pass.

Summer comes and goes; things are usual and reasonable. My mom is breading and selling English Bulldog puppies for income. Larry works as a bus driver for Regional Transit Busses. Granny takes care of us and the house. Larry goes to work every day, and we tend to have family dinners every night. I am happy, and everyone else seems happy too.

I miss Chad, but we talk to him weekly. He is doing well in school and likes having a brother to play with. The dogs are crate trained and stay in the shed in the backyard, which is nice because that many crates would take up a lot of space in the house. She can have ten or more dogs to care for at any given time. I start seventh grade at Joseph Kerr Middle School. Alexia should be starting kindergarten, but my mom does not enroll her. Alexia is a quiet kid and plays well alone. I feel bad for her sometimes since I get to go to school and make friends, but she stays home with Granny all day.

Halloween comes, and I feel like I am too old at 12 to trick or treat, but Granny says she cannot walk that long. Someone needs to take Alexia, and my mom is hiding in her room with Larry again. I do not see them much anymore, but it is okay. So, I take Alexia, dressed as a witch, trick or treating. Granny draws whiskers on my face even though I complain about it. It does make Alexia happy. I have a lot of fun seeing her run up to each house, so excited for a new treat. Larry gets hurt one day on the job, beaten, and robbed. He has to stop working because of this accident. Things change when he is home with my mom all day. We can never do anything right, and we are yelled at all of the time. Whenever they are out of the bedroom, they yell or talk about demons. I am not sure what is going on. My mom is very paranoid, thinking people are out to get her. I do not know what to believe, but I try not to say much as it angers her.

The fighting is more often, and Granny wants my mom to get help for her drug addiction. My mom does not want to. One day Larry throws my mom out and tells her to get help. I am crying, wondering if we must move again since it is Larry's house. A few hours later, there is a knocking on the front door; it is my mom. She is crying at the door, promising to do and be better. Larry lets her come back. She does none of the things she promised. Things get worse. My mother's paranoia affects us all. My windows have been nailed shut, with a lock on the outside of the door. I do not even know what we do to get in trouble most of the time. My mom can find any reason to hurt us, yelling, hair pulling, and more. One day I come home from school. I go to my room to do my homework, and there is a mess of dust in the corner of my room. I look to the ceiling after hearing a loud noise. There is a wire with a camera coming out of the hole in my ceiling. Mom comes down a few minutes later and says the cameras are needed to keep me from leaving, and to prove that I am a demon, out to get her and her unborn baby.

I believe this is the last straw for my grandmother. She is yelling at my mom that she is a crazy drug addict and wants to take Alexia and me out of the house. Granny fears for our safety. Granny threatens to call the police about our treatment. I am not sure what to do or say. This angers my mom so much she is yelling with the lighter clenched between her teeth, spit flying from her mouth as she yells at Granny. Then she and Larry tell Granny she has to move out but cannot take us, kids. Alexia and I are crying, not wanting Granny to go.

My mom pushes Alexia out of her way, and she falls, hitting the wall. I finally break, Alexia got hurt, and our safety net is being thrown out. I yell at my mom. I tell her I hate her and that she is bitch. Before I know what is happening, I am picked up, flung almost upside, and thrown into my bedroom wall. I fall with a loud crash and hurt my arm and shoulder. Afterward, I huddle up in the corner of my room and cry. I am not sure where Alexia is, but I think she is following Granny around while she packs up her stuff and waits for a ride. I do not want her to go. We need her. I am locked in my room while Granny yells at my mom, wanting a chance to say goodbye. I do not get to give Granny a goodbye hug. I can only cry now; I am lying on the floor beside the wall I was tossed against. I write on the wall low to the floor near my dresser, "why does she hate me so much."

Things settle a bit after Granny moves out. I miss school because my mom wants me to stay home and care for Alexia. I do not mind; I love being with her. With Granny gone and Chad living in another state, she truly is my best friend. On the days I go to school, I try to get Alexia up and ready for the day and give her breakfast. I also make sure she can eat the open snacks in my room if she is hungry. Alexia has told me when I am at school; our mom does not feed her. Alexia also says mom and Larry are primarily in their bedroom all day. Going to seventh grade, trying to keep the house clean, get laundry done, and care for my sister is tough. I cry in frustration, and if I say anything to my mom, she yells. She calls me ungrateful. My mom thinks I should do all these things because I have a lovely house and food. I am lonely.

I do not know what happens to Alexia when I am at school, but I do notice changes in her. She never smiles anymore and would not play with her baby dolls anymore. I found them hidden under my bed. I ask her why, and she said that the babies are bad and need a time-out like she gets. I am getting scared, wondering if my parents are putting Alexia in the dark somewhere for a time-out. When I saw her playing, it was only with her stuffed animals, loving them. It is sad knowing Alexia learned from our mom that animals should be treated better than us kids. Both of us have our own special best friend in the form of a dog. I have my rottweiler named Shadow, and Alexia has her German Shepard named Mack. I feel better knowing or hoping the dogs will protect Alexia when I am at school. Unfortunately, the feeling of protection does not last; my mom gets rid of both of our dogs. I am trying to figure out what she did with them. When I ask mom, she says they are demons, too, and we cannot have demon friends.

We get to talk to Granny once in a while. She says she is trying to get us away from mom. One day the police come to the door to do a wellness check on us kids. Alexia says nothing, and I say everything is fine and promise not to miss so much school. What else was I going to say with Larry and my mom standing next to me? The officer never even came into the house; maybe he is not allowed to. The school year is almost over. I will be passing to eighth grade. I am pleased about that. My 13th birthday comes and goes. No one says a thing; they forget all about it. Granny calls though, which was nice. We really miss her. Summer is here, and I am scared. My mom is acting more nuts, always going on about demons and vampires out to get us.

My mom is getting meaner, always calling us names. She is meaner to Alexia, and I do not understand why. I try to take care of her, but if I am too nice to her, my mom takes her anger out on me. Then mom locks me in my room more often. I cannot care for Alexia if I am locked in my room, so I go along with my mom's crazy ideas and meanness. This way, I can be out to care for my sister. I am cleaning the kitchen, and I hear yelling and Alexia crying. I go search for them. I find them in my mom's walk-in closet. They have Alexia tied down to a chair. Legs and arms taped down to the chair limbs. She is hysterical, trying to get loose while my mom cuts off her long dark hair. Telling her how ugly she is now, a nasty Chinese demon. I yell why are you doing this? My mom tells me that Alexia deserves it and that she is tired of taking care of the knots in her long hair. I keep telling my mom to stop and that I will take care of her hair. My mom seems like she is not even hearing me. I get louder to get her to at least let Alexia down from the chair. I guess my mom has enough of my mouth because she reaches up and backhands me in the face. Larry then walks me back to my room and locks me in. I cry because my face is sore and because I cannot help my sister.

Chapter 3

My mom says we are going on a trip to Pennsylvania. Mom says we will go get my brothers back from their dad. She and Larry believe a demon is possessing their dad, and she must save my brothers. We pack up a bag each of the clothes and bathroom stuff we will need. A cooler full of food and drinks is in the back. My mom and Larry take turns driving, and we only stop to get gas and use the bathroom. During the whole drive, there is talk about how we must save the boys from the demons and bring them home. I do not see how she can get Michael back since he was officially adopted, but I do not go against her. The trip there is alright; she is nice to Alexia and me. I am excited to get to Oxford, PA, see Chad, and meet Michael. He is only four, but I have not seen him since he was born. The house we pull up to is like a dream. A long driveway leads to a large two-story home with a dark wooden deck.

Towards the back is another home, this one is a smaller mobile home, but it is still genuinely lovely. There is so much land for us to run and play on—Michael Senior breeds dogs and horses. We get cleaned up in the extra house where we are staying for our trip. Then we kids all get to play together outside. Running all over, petting animals, and using the trampoline. Inside the main house are so many toys. The house even has a train track built to go through the home for Michael to ride. He sits in a little motorized train cart. Both Michael and Chad have gold jewelry. They both seem to be happy and spoiled with their dad. I do not understand why my mom would want to take them away from this kind of life.

Alexia and I stay in the second bedroom of the guest house. She is happier than I have seen her in a long time. Being with our brothers has been good for her. I love seeing her laughing and playing. She wears herself out; it did not take long for her to fall asleep next to me that night. We both wake up before Mom and Larry. We stay quiet, not wanting to disturb them. Waking them up without a good reason is never good for us. Mom and Larry do not think being hungry is a good reason. Mid-morning comes they finally come out of the bedroom. Things have changed; they are cold to Alexia and are being truly short with me. I am nervous; mood changes like this are never good for us. We make our way over to the main house. Larry and my mom go into the kitchen to talk with Michael Sr. alone. The kids take off to play in the yard. Being with all the different animals, we all have so much fun. I would stay forever if I could. We each bundle up into two cars. I ask my mom what is happening, and she says that the boys are safe here with Michael Sr., and he is not a demon. According to my mom, it is us girls that are possessed.

We are going to the lawyer's office to make Chad's adoption official then we are going back to California. The lawyer's office is on the second floor of a small building in a historic-looking town near my brother's house. It is a cute town, within walking distance of many restaurants and little stores. Mom yells at us for being too loud while we play in the office with my brothers. Alexia and Michael are chasing each other around the table in the office. She does not yell at him, just Alexia. Finally, mom grabs Alexia's arm, pulling her down to sit on the floor. All the kids are silent after that, sitting and waiting to be done.

After the grownups finish all the paperwork, we walk down the street to a small diner. All of us get a late breakfast. I overhear Michael Sr. trying to convince my mom to leave us girls with him. Michael Sr. says that he would take care of us. My mom is getting angry, and she refuses his offer. I tell her she should leave Alexia with them, since Chad and Michael are her full siblings. They would be happy together. She snaps at me and makes a scene in the diner. I know I am in big trouble. I remember my place. Good girls listen and are quiet. Things calm down, and we finish breakfast. Getting back to the house Michael Sr. once again tries to convince my mom to leave Alexia, but she ignores him as we pack up the car. We leave the boys behind because they are safe there. The boys are the saviors of the world that need protection to help rid the world of demons and vampires.

The trip back to California seems so much faster but much more terrifying. The whole trip was Larry and mom in the front seat whispering to each other about how to rid us of our demons. I try to sleep and ignore it all. My mom is being extra mean to Alexia. She will not let her sit on the back seat with me. So instead, she stuffs Alexia's small body between the seat and door for most of the 3,000-mile drive back. I want to pull her onto the seat with me, but I know I would get hurt if I did. I feel guilty being mean to Alexia, but I know I have no choice. I just hope she can forgive me.

Chapter 4

We are back home now. It is the beginning of the second week of June 1997. It has been a couple of days since we returned from our trip. I spoke with Granny on the phone, and she worries about us. Honestly, I am too, but I do not know what I can do. I have to listen to my mom or fear the consequences. In the family room, I am feeding Alexia breakfast, and to my surprise, both Larry and my mom are awake. They are never up this early; something is wrong. Our peace of breakfast and cartoons is ruined. Mom and Larry start going on and on about how God informed them how to rid the demons from us. I freeze; I wish I could vanish. This cannot be good, judging by the looks of glee in their eyes. They say they are going to save our souls. According to them, the way to rid us of our demons is to drink bleach milkshakes with other spices included. We have to drink the shake three times a day for eight days. Mom and Larry say they are going to drink them too. The whole family will be saved this way. I take off to my room, taking Alexia's hand in mine; I try to take her with me. Larry stops me from taking her but lets me pass. I hide in my room with the door shut. I know no matter what is to come, that closed door will not help me. I cannot even lock it. There is only a lock from the outside. I can be kept in but cannot keep anyone out. I don't want to drink a bleach milkshake. Drinking a chemical cannot be good; for fucks sake, it tells you not to ingest on the dam bottle. This is bad.

Larry comes to my door a few minutes later. He tells me to go to the kitchen to drink my milkshake. I refuse, backing myself up on my bed as far as I can. I stop when my back and head thuds loudly against the wall. Shit, I have trapped myself. He is becoming more irate the longer I refuse to get up. His dark eyes narrow, pupils wide. He is high. They are always high; I cannot think of anything fast enough to get myself out of this. I feel a flash of guilt just thinking of Alexia out there with mom, what is happening to her. I am too lost in my own fear to do anything about it. Larry is yelling and laughing that I have nowhere to go. Larry says just give up and listen, you damn demon. He comes so close to my face while he yells at me. Larry is calling me awful names while his spittle hits my cheek. He has had enough of my delays. He is so big, towering over me. Before I can gather a thought, he punches me dead in the face between the eyes. Pain radiates all over my face; blood starts to fall from my nose.

"Take that, you fucking demon; get your fat ass in the kitchen now," Larry says. I get up, almost running to the kitchen. I am holding my shirt up to my nose to catch the blood. I do not want to get in more trouble if I make a mess anywhere with my blood. I take a seat at the kitchen table. Larry sits to my right, Alexia to my left, and my mom is right in front of me. I am given a kitchen towel for my nose. Alexia is silently crying; tears roll down her little cheeks. Without a word, I start to dink the bleach shake. It is ridiculously hard since I cannot breathe out of my nose right now.

I keep my eyes open as they dart at each person at the table. Alexia drinks the shake. She is still crying. My nose stops bleeding, and I can finally breathe, although my face really hurts. I am afraid to look at myself. The first sip is horrible. I gag and choke, trying to get it down. Finally, my mom yells to quit the dramatics and drink. She says she drank hers. I highly doubt it. I have not seen either of them take a sip from their cups. The bleach makes my tongue and throat burn, and the coldness of the ice cream does nothing to stop the burn.

My eyes water, and my nose is running. I finally finish the first milkshake. All the while, I am trying to figure out how to get out of the next one. They both seem happy we finished the shakes. Larry and mom leave us at the table. They go back to their bedroom. I am sure to do more drugs. I take this chance and take Alexia to our bathroom. I tell her to be quiet. I turn on the sink to have the sound of the water. I show Alexia how to put her fingers down her throat so she can throw up. I do it myself and rid myself of the bleach. The concoction tastes even worse coming back out. Alexia is not able to figure out how to make herself throw up. I think she is scared. So, I put my fingers down her throat until she finally throws up. We go back to my room and cuddle on the bed. She falls asleep next to me. I wish I could sleep, but I am too scared. I am on the lookout. I listen for any sign they are coming out of their room. I do the math three times a day for eight days means twenty-four bleach shakes. We have one down and twenty-three to go. The rest of the first day goes the same. Alexia and I drink the shakes, and they pretend to. I am able to get us both to throw up each time that day.

The following day fear wakes me up. I get up and do all of my everyday chores. I get Alexia, and I ready for the day. After breakfast, we play with playdoh while cartoons are on. Larry and mom wake up mid-morning. As soon as they see us, they yell at us to keep away. They tell us how awful we are and that the demons will be gone soon. None of this makes any sense to me. I just keep my mouth shut; we have our breakfast shake. We get away to go throw up, but mom catches us in the act. Her hands are flying all over the place, slap after slap to both of us. We are huddled behind the bathroom door. I use my body to cover Alexia the best that

I can. We are both taken to our rooms, the clicking of the lock is the only sound I hear for the rest of the day. We are taken out to have our shakes at separate times now. I messed up getting us caught; things will get worse, I know it. I cannot imagine how things could get any worse, but my mom always finds a way. The following day there is no getting up and getting ready as I am locked in my room. This makes me more fearful, thinking about the fact that the only way out of the room is if they let me out. I am scared to think what new torture lies ahead.

It's the third day of the exorcism. Six shakes down, eighteen to go. I am finally brought out of my room and allowed to use the bathroom. I go to the kitchen. Alexia is up and had her shake already. I force mine down; they get worse tasting each time. I think my mom is adding more bleach to them. Larry sits at the table. His hands are on the tabletop his fist keeps clenching like he is preparing to fight.

I will not go against them anymore; my face is still sore, and I still have two black eyes. I do not want a repeat of Larry punching me. I try to get close to Alexia to check on her but am pushed aside. Luckily, I fall onto the couch, so I do not get hurt this time. My mom takes Alexia in her lap. My mom goes to sit on the brown recliner. On the side table is a cup and what looks like a medicine dropper. I break out in a cold sweat. What is happening now, shit this must be some punishment for fighting back. Larry sits next to me on the couch. I try to inch away but am met with the arm of the sofa, shit nowhere to go. I do not run. I do not call for help. I would not make it far anyway. Larry is giddy. Time to get these demons out, he says. I say isn't that what the bleach shakes are for? I think they are working. I am feeling better. My mom bursts out laughing good try, demon whore, that will not work with us.

Now watch your turn is next. My turn for what? Then I hear Alexia; a scream leaves her mouth. It is the most terrifying sound I have ever heard. Mom shoves a rag in her mouth to silence her. I watch in horror as she uses the dropper to put bleach in Alexia's eyes and ears. Once done with her, mom pushes Alexia off her to the floor. Alexia does not move. She just looks towards the wall, all tears, snot, and muffled sobs. The next thing I know, Larry pins me to his chest while my mom uses the dropper to put bleach in my ears and eyes. I do not even flinch or try to get away. I know it is no use. Larry is too big and strong. I feel weak, like a coward. The pain is too much. I must pass out for a short time. I awaken. I lay on my side on the couch, eyes burning and ears ringing. Startled, I look around for Alexia and do not see her anywhere. I am worried for her but feel a tiny bit of relief at being alone for a while. I go to the bathroom to wash my eyes and clean up. I still do not see or hear Alexia,

I am worried, but I do not go to look for her. I know better. I make something to eat and watch TV. The rest of the day is long. After two more shakes, we cannot throw up, but at least the dropper stays away from us for now. I hope this treatment was a one-time thing.

Day four of the exorcism, nine shakes down fifteen to go. Today is much of the same. We both get our bleach shakes, and a dropper full of bleach to our ears and eyes. They have kept Alexia and I apart more too. I am worried about what they are doing to her. What are the things I cannot see? Not like it matters; I am too weak to do anything about it. Calling the police would do nothing. They have been here before and left us anyway. The police left believing the lies they were told. I cannot get to the phone anyway, and they keep it away from me. I will not leave and try to make a run for it because I will not leave Alexia behind. I cannot leave her; she is all I have. According to my mom, Granny does not love us anymore. Granny now sees us for the demons we are. I do not want to believe my mom, but she will not let me talk to Granny.

Day five of the exorcism twelve shakes down twelve to go. Day five is the same as yesterday, besides an added bonus. Well, according to my mom, anyway. She calls me outside to the backyard. It is the first time I have been outside in a week. It is a beautiful day. The sun is out, birds are singing, no clouds in the sky. I am jealous of the birds flying free. I want to be free too. But I see no way out. My mom yells, snapping me out of my daydream. My mom calls me back to the farthest corner of the yard, where we have grass and shade trees. My mom is there. She smells of menthol cigarettes, a lighter hanging from her mouth, missing teeth, hair chopped short, and roots growing out. She looks so old under the outdoor light. She shows me a giant red plastic bucket with two white rope handles. It is filled with bleach water. I want to be sick. What is she going to do to us this time?

She smiles down at me, says this is not for you this time. With a laugh, she has me go to the shed and get one of our dogs. She takes the Bulldog and puts her face first in the bucket of water. My mom holds her head down until she stops moving. I am in shock. My mom just drowned an innocent dog. The same dogs she loves more than her kids. My mom tells me demons possess the dogs too. Mom says they need to die. She says I can expect the same if the exorcism does not work. She has to save her baby. What baby? She says she is pregnant.

I do not believe her, but I do not care anyway. I have other things to worry about. My mom makes me bring out each and every dog one by one. The dogs go to her tails wagging, wanting love. They walk to their death without a fight; why would they? The dogs love her. She has always cared for them. I am made to bring these dogs to their painful end. Hell, a bird flying low is not even safe from my mother. She takes a spray bottle of bleach, dosing the bird until he dies too. I have to march over ten dogs I love to their deaths. This is just another way for my mom to get to me. I listen and do as I am told; a good girl always does.

Day six of the exorcism fifteen shakes down nine to go. Shakes and drops are today's agenda. I go outside to the backyard. I see no signs of the torture that took place. It is like nothing happened aside from the small patch of grass that is yellowing and dead, and the empty dog crates in the shed. I would not ever know anything was different. I do not get to see Alexia today. I am scared for her. I did hear her crying, so at least I know she is still alive. Sometimes I wish for death. It has to be easier and less painful.

Day seven of the exorcism eighteen shakes down six to go. We have our breakfast shake at the table. Alexia does not look well. She is pale and not moving or responding much. She is having a hard time getting her milkshake down. This angers my mom; she drags Alexia out of the room by her hair. I barely hear a whimper out of Alexia as she is dragged away. Mom locks her in her bedroom closet. I am allowed to do whatever I want after my shake. I ask to see Alexia. I am denied. It is time for our lunchtime shake. I am sitting at the table. I wait for Alexia to join. She never does; I hear noise and look behind me. The light to the hall bathroom is on. My mom calls for Larry to help her. I am made to follow. Alexia is in the bathtub, there is no water, but she is naked, and there is a red enema bag in the tub with her. I am not allowed in the bathroom, Larry and my mom whisper to each other. I try to focus on their words, but I cannot. I am worried that Alexia is dead. I focus on her, I can see her chest rising, and she does let out a tiny sigh. I am relieved she is still alive. Larry pulls me back to the kitchen table; I am told to sit and finish my shake. He watches me intently. I am almost done with my shake when my mom calls Larry. I look towards the bathroom. I see my mom. She kneels on the floor next to my sister's naked, lifeless body. I am frozen I do not move a muscle or make a sound. My mom leans down and places her ear to Alexia's chest. I wait. Mom keeps her ear to her chest, saying nothing. Mom comes up and tries giving Alexia CPR. She does not try long. A sob leaves my chest. They do not notice. Two breaths are all my mom does, no chest compressions, nothing. I want to yell for my mom to call an ambulance, but I do not. I take one more look over, and my mom is smiling, looking down at Alexia. That is when I know for sure my sister is dead, and my mom is happy about it. Larry seems a little more shaken up about it all, worrying about what to do with her body. I feel as if I am drowning. My head hurts, and my ears are ringing, but I hear nothing. I feel, and feeling is terrible. The next thing I see is Larry putting Alexia's body in a large black trash bag. Is he just going to put her body in the trash? No, that would not be smart. Larry takes her body and places her into the deep freezer in the garage. I want to yell are you sure she is dead and cannot be saved? She will not be able to breathe in that bag in the freezer. I again say nothing. Fear keeps me quiet. They have killed so they could do it again.

Day eight of the exorcism, but no shakes are given. Instead, my mom and Larry are being genuinely nice to me. They feed me my favorite food and allow me access to the house instead of being locked in my room. The niceness scares me more than anything else. Mom and Larry talk about what to do with Alexia's body. I hate being asked to go to the garage to get a soda knowing my sister is in that freezer. Two days go by with lots of talking. I try to keep out of the way. I hope I will not have to be a part of their plan for my sister's body. Unfortunately, I do not think I will get that lucky.

Chapter 5

What time is it? I am warm and sweaty lying in bed. I wish I could open the window. Fat chance since it is bolted shut. Where do they think I am going to go? Is it to keep me in or keep people out? She says there are people after us. The cameras in my ceiling record them. I have asked to see the tapes; she always ignores me or changes the subject. I am lonely. It is too quiet. I wish she would not have kicked my Granny out of the house. I miss Alexia. I have not said her name in days. The last time I did, mom smacked me in the face and to me to shut up. The demons took Alexia's body, and her soul was gone.

I do not believe my mom, but I keep quiet. What if she is telling me the truth? Moms do not lie, do they? I keep my radio low; I do not want to wake them. Maybe I can sneak to the kitchen for a snack. I am hungry. Shit, the door is locked too. Back to bed, I go. All I can do is lay here and think. Thinking does no good. I need to pee, but if I wake them, they will be mad. I doze off again with nothing else to do. Panicked, I wake up. I hear them talking, coming to my door.

I stay quiet. My mom opens the door and tells me to go eat something. I use the bathroom and get some lunch. I do not taste my food; I devour my food before they can tamper with it. I eat too fast and choke. Larry yells, "what is wrong with you? Stop eating like a pig." I say nothing and finish eating. I make use of the bathroom again just in case they are going to lock me back in my room. The bathroom door slams open. I yelp in fear. They are both there, staring at me. It is like they are staring into my soul. I am scared but stay quiet. My eyes bounce from my mom to Larry and back, trying to prepare for whoever makes the first move. Larry moves his hand from behind his back. I flinch back. I think he is going to hit me. Oh, shit, it is worse. He shows me a gun. What now?

I am told to go to the master bedroom closet. My mom is ahead of me, Larry behind with the gun. I walk, and I try to slow down. Larry pushes the gun to my lower back and tells me to move. I do. I am guided to the walk-in closet. I am forced inside. My mom is already in the closet. Larry blocks the closet doorway, still holding the gun. I almost slip while I am wearing socks, and I look down. Plastic garbage bags are lining the closet floor, and I realize that is why I slipped. Weird what happened to the clothes in the closet? My mom moves aside. I look down again and see knives, a pruning saw, and what looks like a small ax-type thing, and the entire black trash bag. I recheck the only exit; Larry still blocks it with the gun in hand. I do not know why I keep looking. I know even if I wanted to escape, I could not. If I did get past him, the bad guys my mom told me about would abduct me to hurt me, then bring me home. I stay quiet and stare at the black trash bag. I know what is in that bag. I am still quiet. I am waiting for either of them to say something or do something. This waiting is terrible.

My mom cuts open the black trash bag. I look anywhere but at the bag. Larry notices; he yells at me to watch and tells me I will be next if I do not do as I am told. I look at the cut-open bag tears form in my eyes, but I do not let them fall. I am numb. Looking down, I see her curled up like a baby sleeping on her side. I know better. She will not be waking up. I am angry they cut her long dark hair. They made her look like a boy. Why am I mad over hair when I am staring at the lifeless body of my little sister? It does not matter to me she is still beautiful; she is now my beautiful angel. I feel bad. I am also angry at her; she got to escape. Angels go to heaven. I wish for heaven sometimes too.

I am startled out of my thoughts. My mom gets a new cigarette; the smoke fills the closet. Larry holds the shining metal of the gun up to my head, says watch, listen, and remember, if I do not, I will end up just like Alexia. A frozen body in a trash bag that no one will remember. I just nod, and I do not say anything. If I say one wrong word, he will shoot me. I know he will. I wait. For a moment, she looks unsure; she starts talking too fast for me to understand. Her words make no sense. Finally, Larry gets angry and tells her to take the gun and keep it towards me. I am lost. What is happening now? Larry looks at my mom and says I will start, and then you must finish. Is it just me, or does my mom look scared, too? The look is gone before I can register it.

She is not frightened. She is high again. Larry takes the pruning saw and places it on Alexia's frozen neck. Faster than I would have thought possible, he uses the pruning saw to remove her head from the rest of her body.

Seeing this, my mom seems prepared for what I do not know. Larry takes the gun back from my mom and aims it at me. "Watch and listen; you got it," Larry yells. I nod. It seems as if time stands still, and my legs get tired. I guess Larry's does, too. He yells, sit. We both take a seat, me in the corner of the closet as close to the exit as I can get without touching Larry. He sits cross-legged in the closet doorway. Gun in hand, laying on his lap, still pointing at me. I pull my legs up to my chest and hug my knees. I am watching and listening like I was told to do. I listen. I always listen. It is safer that way. Larry repeatedly says that if anyone asks where Alexia is, I will tell them she lives with her father in Chicago. I nod and repeat when he asks me to. It is hot, but I wish I did not wear shorts and a tank top. Sweat rolls down my back and behind my knees. I do not move. Hours pass, the stench of the closet getting worse each minute that goes by.

Her body is thawing, and the smell of death is oozing from her. I want to be sick, but I say nothing. I watch like I was told. Good girls, listen. I want to rub my legs clean; I want a shower. I sit still and say nothing as pieces of my sister's body, skin, muscle, and bone fly through the air with the force of my mom's chopping. Bits of Alexia stick to my exposed skin. Startled when my mom announced she was done. I finally see. Even though I was watching, I did not truly see. What happened to my sister? Then, of course, another trash bag, this one full of Alexia in oatmeal-like consistency. I say nothing. I sit and watch. I wish for heaven too.

Chapter 6

I do not understand what is happening. Outside, the rest of the world is enjoying a beautiful summer day. It is the third week of July; I like to imagine family trips to the fair or swimming somewhere. We never do anything like I see families do on TV. I always wonder if other families live like mine or if they are more like I see in movies. I am lost in a daydream when my mom tells me to take a shower. I rush to the bathroom, start the shower, strip off and climb in. I hate this bathroom; the stall feels too small. I feel like I cannot breathe. The walls are crashing down around me. Scalding water wants to drown me. I want to let it. I cannot get clean enough. I still feel dirty. I do not think I will ever get clean. It is not lost to me that I am washing away bits of skin, blood, and bone in the same tub/shower where Alexia took her last breath. How can I get clean in a place so tainted? The water is getting cold. I need to hurry. I do not want to know what comes next. I still do not cry. Crying gets me punished.

Coming out of the bathroom, I try to escape quickly to my room. Bolted windows and locked doors are safer. I smell lighter fluid. Did they light the barbecue? Are we having lunch? I do not feel like eating. I am almost in my room when my mom calls for me. Damn, even if I made it to my room, I would have to listen to her and come out. I can never escape them. I follow her voice and find them in the family room; the fireplace is lit. I have never seen a fire so large or felt one so hot. It is too hot in the room, and the air conditioning cannot keep up. My mom sits on the loveseat and beckons me to sit with her. She hands me a bowl of ice cream. She has one too. She is laughing and happy and tells me to eat. She bought Mint Chip just for me." I wanted to get you your favorite, a nice treat," she states. My mom is right. Usually, that is my favorite, but not right now. I am sick at the thought of eating anything. But I take the spoon, bring it to my mouth and eat the ice cream with a small smile and a thank you. The ice cream tastes like chalk and does not want to go down. I force it. I keep eating bite after bite until that bowl is clean. My mom hugs me close and tells me she loves me. I do not say anything back; I can see she is getting angry at my lack of response. I force the words I love you too out of my dry, cracked lips. That brings her back to a state of happiness. I never know what version of mom I will get.

Larry says he thinks the fire is hot enough now. I am lost. Hot enough for what? He brings over the filled black trash bag. Larry opens it up and grabs a large handful. He tosses it into the fire. He watches like it is the best action movie he has ever seen, too involved to look away. Not wanting to miss a moment of the action. Time moves slowly. Larry gets frustrated. "I will have to toss in smaller amounts and keep the fire as hot as possible," he tells my mom. Time stands still. The odors start assaulting my nose. I keep breathing through my mouth. After a few minutes, he sends another handful of what used to be my 5-year-old little sister into the flames. Dark black smoke flies up the chimney. Barbara lights some candles and uses an air freshener. The scents do nothing to mask the fumes of a burning body. Overusing the air freshener makes it all worse my eyes are burning and watering. Still, I stay quiet and watch the flames.

The flames are magnificent, my sister's final goodbye. Her soul is sent via the smoke to the heavens. That is what I tell myself, but I say nothing to my mom and Larry. They chat back and forth about what I will never know. I stopped hearing. Just eyes focused on the bag of my sister's remains and the flames. Eyes move left to right and back as each handful of remains finds its way into the fire. Huh, no gloves. I focus on Larry's hand reaching into the bag, no gloves. No gloves, no gloves, no gloves, is repeatedly in my head. That is gross. How can he do that? I should not even ask if they killed a child and dismembered her. Not wearing gloves is nothing to him. But I remain focused on his tan hand, no gloves, into the bag and back to the fire. I feel as if time has stopped, but it does not. I wish it would.

It is a surprisingly fast process to burn her completely. Maybe because she was so small, or because they decimated her body so thoroughly. I am finally allowed to go back to my room. Closing the door, I climb into my bed and hide under my covers. I know it is not safe. No spot in this house is safe. I am stuck in this house. I have never wished for school to start so much. I am terrified I will end up like Alexia and not see my eighth-grade year. I should feel lucky even to have gotten through 7th grade when she was never allowed to attend kindergarten. Closing my eyes, I wish for my Granny. I do not pray. God never listens anyway.

Light knocking on my door wakes me up. I must have fallen asleep. I pull the cover off my head. My room is dark; I must have slept for a while if it is dark outside now. Jess, get up and get some shoes on. We are going out. Inside I panic, going where to do what? I want to go back under the covers. I do as I am told; I always do it is safer that way. We all make our way to the driveway to my mom's white Bronco. She loves that car and likes it when driving; people are yelling GO OJ. Why did she have to buy the same type of car as OJ Simpson for attention? My mom always wants things about her. I busy my mind worrying about dumb things like her car choice. It is much safer than thinking about what happened today or what might happen to me. Yes, the white Bronco and the OJ trial are safer.

In the back seat, I chose the center seat, which had a better view of them both. It is dark, and we have been driving for a while now. I think they may be lost. It might be a better way to die being lost by the Sacramento River. We finally stop. The weather is cooler; it is very dark along the river. The water is loudly rushing away to meet a larger body of water. I want to jump in. I want the river to take me away. I do not run away. I do not jump in the water. I am terrified. Too scared to run away to the unknown. If I stay, I know them and the crazy we live. I have handled it before. The unknown is worse right now. They pick a spot along the river. A mess of trees, mud, and miles of nothing around. Larry goes to the back of the Bronco, opens the hatch, and takes out a small red cooler with a white lid. It looks like one he used for his lunches when he was working. Why does he have it out now?

I watch as Larry takes the cooler to the water's edge. He slips a bit on the mud. How I wish he would fall in. Opening the cooler, he tosses the white lid, and turns the red cooler upside down. I watch, now knowing why we are here. This is her final resting place. The ashes slowly fall out of the cooler into the breeze floating down to land on the water. She is gone. There is nothing left. He lets the cooler go, and my mom hands him the tools they used to dismember her. Those get tossed in the river too. They both smile as they watch the items float a bit and sink, being taken far away. I want to go with her.

Walking the short distance back to the car, the doors will not open. My mom locked the keys in the car. I tremble in fear. She is getting angry. They are starting to fight. This cannot be good. Larry takes a rock and breaks the back window allowing him to reach the locks. Crisis averted, this time. Before I know it, we are back home, it is late, and

I am tired. I head off to bed and place the covers overhead.

Wishing for a way out but never praying for one.

Chapter 7

I really try not to think about Alexia and her death. Pretending all is well, is what keeps me going. I have thought of many ways to kill myself. I would rather take my own life than let my mother do it. She would get too much satisfaction from it. I lock myself in the bathroom, sitting on the floor by the sink with every chemical I can find, by my feet. I think of drinking them all. The combination would surely kill me, right? The only cleaner I did not bring with me is bleach. The smell alone makes me sick. I just cannot bring myself to kill myself. I cannot let them win. I do not know how to escape this hell, but they cannot win. Plus, I cannot hurt Granny like that. My mom lets me talk to her occasionally, only with her listening in. I am terrified each and every day since Alexia died, but this is a different kind of fear. They both are being nice, and that makes it worse. I understand mean yelling and ignoring me. Friendly, not so much. I know that no matter how good I am; things will go bad again.

A couple of weeks after Alexia died, the cops came to the door to do a wellness check on us kids. Once again, I tell them I am safe and well. I also make sure to tell them that Alexia is in Chicago with her father. Even if Larry and my mom were not standing next to me, blocking the doorway, and keeping the cops out, I would have told them that story. No way would I go against them. I would be killed for sure. The police officers leave. I do not think they believed me, but they still had to leave. Things change after that visit from the police, even though I was good, and told them what my mom told me to. I do not know what I did to mess up. The meanness that used to be directed at Alexia is now all directed at me.

The talk of possession, demons, and vampires is an all-day, everyday thing. At this point, I go along with the conversation just to keep them happy. My mom is mean to me. Not physically, but with her words, she knows how to make me feel like shit. Every day without fail, I am told how ugly, fat, and stupid I am. One day she calls me from the living room to the family room. There is a small fire in the fireplace. My mom rants about how I think I am so bright and better than her. I am confused. I was just watching TV. What did I do now? I finally notice the white box she has. It was in my closet. That box is full of all my memories, report cards, letters, awards, and things that mean a lot to me. That box is all I have of good memories. I beg her to let me have it back. She laughs and puts the whole package in the fire. I am sobbing, trying to reach into the fire to get my special box back. She grabs me by my hair, forces me onto my knees, and makes me watch until it is all nothing but ash. I know that no matter what, I will never be good enough for her to love, but still, I do whatever I can to get her to love me. I will not go against her, I love her, but I am not sure I should.

Larry and my mom are redoing the floors in the master bedroom. Larry has some friends over to help with the tear-out. It is two teen boys a few years older than me. I am guessing 15-16. Larry and my mom leave me alone with these young men. I try to get to my room and lock the door. I am not fast enough. They tell me Larry said that I would be their payment for helping remove the carpet. Before I know it, I am naked on the bed with them touching me all over. I keep batting their hands away. They are laughing. Telling me I am too fat and ugly to be a worthwhile payment. Larry and my mom come to the door laughing and tell the boys Okay, enough, you had your fun. Let us get back to work. I scramble to get my clothes back on. I shut and lock the door and cry.

The rest of the summer is more of the same. I am starting to believe all the things they call me. The newest bull is that I am pregnant with Larry's brother's baby. My mom made me pee on a stick and everything. I keep telling her she is wrong and that I have never even kissed a boy. Finally, she yells at me to shut up, demon, leaving with the pregnancy test in hand. She swears it is positive talking with Larry. Then she calls Larry's brother's wife to inform her of his affair and the baby on the way. So many lies and drama. I do not understand any of it.

Another night I am called into the master bedroom made to drink a cup of tea. I found out later that night that she put meth in my drink to see what would happen to me. I am glad nothing happened; I did not get high. Maybe she didn't use enough or digesting instead of smoking changes how it affects you. I got lucky that night. I fear what they would have done to me if I did get high, maybe call Larry's friends back. Another night I am made to get naked and get in the hot tub with them. I try to cover myself, but Larry and his needy eyes see all. He even makes a comment about my pubic hair. School finally starts back up. I was worried they would not let me go. But Larry reminds my mom that the police officers would look for me if I did not attend school. I am glad he had a moment of sanity. School is the only place I am safe. School is the only place I can be normal.

Chapter 8

I made it through another day of eighth grade.
School is my safe place; I wish I would never have to leave.
But, when I walked in the door that afternoon, all was
normal. My parents are locked away in their room, and I am
left to care for myself. I go to my room to start my
homework. I hear muffled voices coming from the back of
the bedroom. My stomach turns, and I feel ill. I wonder what
version of mommy will come from behind that locked door.
Woo, I am in luck they do not appear. I quickly make myself
dinner and return to my room with the door shut and locked.
The evening passes, and I get ready for bed.

I am sleeping soundly, well as soundly as one can in
the house of demons. I am startled when I wake up. My

mother swings open my door, yelling words I do not understand due to still being partly asleep. All I can keep thinking is shit, and I forgot to lock the door. My mom allowed me to have an inside lock on my door after Alexia died. My parents allowed this because they wanted me to have a false sense of security. That way, I would keep up the lies they wanted me to share. While Larry is behind her, lurking and not saying a word, my mother is still going on incoherently. I do not know who to fear more; loud and crazy or quiet and crazy.

I am finally awake and can understand what is being yelled at me. "Get up, GET UP, go sleep in the shed, NOW," mom yells. I am confused, "what did I do this time," I ask. I am lost, it is the middle of the night, and once again, I am being told to sleep in the backyard shed. I never understand what I have done to have to be banished from the house again. "You demon get out; I can't have you kill my unborn baby," my mom yells. I say nothing. I am not sure how to respond. It could be worse for me if I agree that I am a demon. But, if I disagree, I will anger her more because I am "lying." I did not ask any questions. Instead, I gather my backpack, school clothes, and blanket. I quickly make my way outside to the backyard shed. My mom lurks behind me to ensure I go where I am told. All the while, she tells me I am a demon trying to suck the electricity out of her baby.

In the shed, it is dark. The only light comes from the moon into the small window inside the shed. I look around inside. There is a long white lounge chair. I lay my blanket down. I sit, and all I see are many empty dog kennels. I think back to all the English Bulldogs we once had, and then my mind flashes to how my mother drowned them all in a bucket of bleach water. But, I know to listen, and do as I am told. She has repeatedly proven what could happen to me if I disobey or disagree, even though she has not verbally warned me.

The shed feels cold; it is damp, gray, and lonely. I am glad it is still warm outside, it being the end of summer. I feel like the four walls of the shed are slowly moving inwards, boxing me in. I know they are not, but I feel suffocated. Realizing I have to pee, what do I do? I do not dare go back into the house to use the bathroom. I see a five-gallon bucket that we use to store dog supplies in. I make do in the situation I am in. I make my way in the dark a few feet back to the lawn chair. Grab my blanket, curl up, and pray to fall asleep. The chair is hard, and I cannot get comfortable. I want to return to the house, to my warm bed, and lock the bedroom door.

I feel myself drift off to sleep, hoping that morning comes quickly so I can be off to school, where I am safe and happy. The dreams begin of happier times; I can breathe easily and relax. Then out of nowhere, I am once again startled awake, this time by the sound of a heavy wood door as it slams against the many dog crates. Wood against metal rings in my ears. I sit up quickly. Confused with my blurred eyes, I try to adjust to the minimal light in the shed. I hear voices. I try to focus. Muffled words become clear. "Time to rid her of the demons. It is not safe to have her here," Barbara exclaims. I am frightened. What in the hell does rid the demons mean? Then splashes of warm liquid fall from my head, dripping down my body. Larry states, "you like that, don't ya." I shoot up to my feet, another toss of liquid. I am in a daze. I realize by the scent that Larry has tossed bleach on me. I still say nothing. The door is closed. There I am, alone and wet. The scent of bleach is so strong I feel sick. My skin gets hot; I feel a sensation of burning along my head, shoulders, back, and thighs. I do not know what to do; all I know is my whole body hurts. I grab my blanket for comfort.

That, too is mostly soaked in bleach. I curl up in the fetal position with the part of the blanket that is dry. I cry, cry, and cry, not making a sound. I drift off for a brief time. It is hard to sleep. I am afraid and in pain. Why is the morning taking so long to come?

I feel a breeze enter the shed; I realize the gush of air is from the door opening. I cringe. I wish I could hide. I wish I were somewhere else. What is going to happen now? Then I feel it. The ice-cold water sends chills down my spine. No words are said. I am bathed with a couple of minutes of freezing water. I am drenched. The door is closed. I am alone again. After the initial shock and coldness wears off, I welcome the spray down. The water eases my pain from the bleach burns all over my body. I dry off the best that I can. I want to change into my school clothes, but I need them to be clean and dry. Who knows if my mother will return before the night ends? I curl up in the chair again, this time cold and wet, but at least the pain is a bit less due numbing effect of the chilly water. The alarm goes off; it is time to get ready for school. I am relieved. I grab my clothes for school; I am disappointed some bleach splatters made it onto my clean pants. The bottom hem of my jeans has bleach spots where the color is fading. I hope it is not too noticeable. I do not go into the house. I am hungry and would like to brush my teeth. I do not dare disturb the beasts that lay resting in the house of demons. I instead hop on my bike and pedal as fast as I can to school.

The feeling of freedom and momentary safety leaves me feeling that things might be OK. Unfortunately, the relief does not last. With each pedal of the bike, my pain increases. It feels as if my skin is tearing centimeter by centimeter. There is no relief from the pain of the bleach burns. I still have a couple of miles to school, and then it hits me; my first class is gym; how am I will I be able to participate in gym to the

-to-toe painful burns? I scramble to of gym class. When I get to school, I the school office. With each step, pain radiates in ... act parts of my body. I notice that I can still smell the bleach in my hair. My hair changes color as the hours go on and my hair is very stiff. I wonder if people will notice. I wonder if they do will they say anything? How will I answer the questions? In the office, I request to be excused from gym glass. I tell them I fell in bleach; they misunderstand and think I said I fell off the bleachers and hurt myself. I go with that. At least I do not have to participate in gym. I would never change in front of people with burns. I cannot hide them in a t-shirt and gym shorts. I am relieved I can sit down this school period.

I go from class to class, trying to make it through the day unnoticed. I know that I smell and that the bleach is eating away the bottoms of my jeans, yet I strive to make it through the day. I cannot miss the standardized testing. My mother would surely kill me if I was ever caught missing school. I can only miss school when she allows it. I would never go against her rules. She scares me too much. At lunch, I finally get to eat. I am starving. I talk with my friend Jamie; she thinks I should tell someone that it is unsafe for me to go home. Deep down, I know she is correct, but my mom will be so angry and kill me if I told on her. I am once again confused. I continue through the school day. My burns are so painful; I would love to take a shower; to get the scent of bleach off me. Finally, I make it to my last period of the day, Mrs. Cooper's math class. I must make a choice now or never. Tell someone I cannot go home or go home and face whatever may meet me.

I walk into my sixth-period class, and at that moment, I know I CANNOT go home. I walk up to Mrs. Cooper and tell her I cannot go home. As my classmates file in, I take my seat. I try to focus during the hour-long class. The bell finally rings, and the students clear out. I tell Mrs. Cooper what my parents have done. I can see many different emotions on her face. I wonder if I made the wrong choice. What happens now? Mrs. Cooper and I talk for a time. Finally, she calls another teacher into the classroom. We make our way to the office. Mrs. Cooper talks with other grownups. I am more confused now than before.

Are they calling my parents? Do they believe me? If I must go home directly after telling people, I am sure I will not live another day to tell anyone else. Then Mrs. Cooper comes to me with a camera in her hand; why does she need that? "Jess, I need to take pictures of your burns," Mrs. Cooper says. I am nervous that my burns are in private areas; I do not want anyone to see me without clothes or underwear. I feel sick again. What did I do? I should have just gone home. If I go now, my parents will know something is happening, and I will be in trouble for coming home late. I am screwed. We go into the staff restroom, I partly undress, and Mrs. Cooper takes pictures of my burns. Behind the lenses of the camera, her eyes are sad, like she wants to cry. I do not cry.

The police are called. I again have to tell more people what happened. I do not care for all these strangers. I wonder if my parents know that I have told on them yet. Are they mad? Should I care if they are? I just want to see my Granny. I miss her. If my mom had not kicked her out of the house, she could have helped me. The police say I need to go to the hospital to be checked out by doctors. I do not understand why. I am fine. All I need is a shower and clean clothes. I do not want to go with the police officers alone. I fear they will take me home. I have so many thoughts, and I cannot make sense of them all. I think maybe all families are like mine. I hope not. Mrs. Cooper says she will stay with me. I am relieved. She rides in the back of the police car with me to the hospital. I have never been in a police car; I notice there are no door latches to open the door. I am scared. I hate confined spaces. It is hard to breathe. Mrs. Cooper and I talk about her kids. I am glad we are talking about something other than me. My mind wanders; I fantasize about what having a good mother would be like.

In the hospital, I am taken to a room with a shower. Things are happening so quickly. Mrs. Cooper is in another room; she promises she will not leave. I am unsure if I believe her; in my experience, adults do not tell the truth and are not there for me even a little. I am instructed to undress and given a hospital gown. Mrs. Cooper comes into the exam room. She stayed like she said she would. A woman doctor examines me. I am glad she is a girl, especially when she tells me she has to examine my private parts. I do not understand why she must look down there. I let her. I am taken to a room with a shower. I wait to be alone. An officer comes in, and she wants to take pictures of me naked. I ask why? She says they are evidence of my abuse and burns. I do as I am told, mostly because I want a shower. I am glad the officer is a woman. She takes pictures, and I get to be clean. I am given a clean gown and brought out; I sit next to Mrs. Cooper. I am grateful she is still here. She has not left me yet. I wonder what will happen next.

Without many words, Mrs. Cooper and I are in the back of the police car again. I am tired. No one tells me what is going to happen next. We pull up to a large building. The officer lets us out. The sign reads The Children's Receiving Home of Sacramento; what have I gotten myself into? We go inside and take a seat on what looks like a gray doctor waiting room chairs. It is late. Mrs. Cooper is staying with me. I am told I am going back for intake. Mrs. Cooper and I say our goodbyes. She promises to visit and to keep in contact. I wonder if she means it. I walk down a long hallway to heavy double doors. I am taken to the dorms; I am in Willows One for girls twelve and older. I meet the night staff Barbara. Once again, I am asked to shower, and Barbara marks down where my burns are on her intake sheet. I am really tired of having to be naked in front of people. I am given clean pajamas and shown to my room. I feel lucky; I have a single room. I am finally allowed to go to bed. I climb under the covers; millions of thoughts run through my head. Then I realize I am alone again.

Chapter 9

The receiving home is supposed to be temporary care for around 30 days until the social workers can find a placement in a foster home. The CRH is all bright overhead lights, hard linoleum floors, and long hallways. The setup reminds me of a hospital with different units for different kinds of illnesses. The difference is each unit in the CRH is called a dorm, and they hold kids grouped by age and gender, and the sickness treated is abuse. The place is not home-like, even though it looks like they tried. The first things that happen in the receiving home are many court dates, social worker visits, and interviews with the police. It is a mess.

Learning the rules of the home, going to school in the same building, and dealing with the abuse from my parents is too much. One social worker had me read my mother's statement to the police. She said she did not want me and wants me to die in her statement. I read the words and know they are true, but I do not cry. The receiving home is nothing like living at home. There are so many rules. I have to ask to make phone calls, I cannot leave the premises without being checked out, and I have to get visitors approved by the social worker before they can see me. I do not understand it all. I only want to be able to talk to my Granny and Mrs. Cooper. One thing I hate is the no-soda rule. I miss having a soda when I want to.

October 7, 97, was the first time I was allowed to talk to my Granny. She called just before dinner. She says she is trying to get an apartment, so I can go live with her. I would love to live with her. I miss her. Waiting for the social worker to approve everything is hard. I cannot wait until I can see my Granny and Mrs. Cooper. I find it funny that my teacher is becoming my best friend. I have finally settled into a routine here at the receiving home, with school and all the different rules. I am unhappy with still being here, but I am happy to be safe. My visitor list is finally approved. On October 10, 97, I was finally able to have a visit. Mrs. Cooper and my Granny got to take me off the grounds. We went to Mcdonald's, and I finally got my diet coke.

Living in the receiving home is a significant adjustment. Days are full of rules and schedules. I do not understand all of the rules, and it seems like too much to me. We eat only in the cafeteria area during scheduled meal and snack times. It is odd not being able to go to the kitchen to get food or drinks whenever I want, as I did at home. I did when I knew Larry and my mom was in their room. TV is limited at times and shows too. I am upset that I cannot watch the soap operas I love; Granny says she will record them for me. Plus, we cannot watch the news at all. The staff says it is because they do not want the kids to see their cases on TV. Something about emotional safety and all. I am not allowed to go to a real school. Class is held at the receiving home. Apparently, they are authentic teachers, and the coursework counts, so I will not be held back or anything. I do not want this mess to affect me going to high school. We also have to do chores, allowing us to earn points to spend in the point store. I guess it is the homes version of allowance. When I first got to the CRH, I had to get clothes from the dorm closet. It sucks having to wear other people's clothes, which are not cute. I could not wait to get my own clothes and things so I would not have to share with 12 other girls. That is, on average, how many kids are in each dorm, and we are separated by age groups. I am in Willows One for girls 12 to 17.

I was shocked to see girls my age with big pregnant bellies. I had never met a pregnant teen before. The older girls, around 15 and older, all the girls talk about is boys, sex, and drugs. It seems like too much to be worried about while being in temporary care. I am more worried about if my mom will get help and where I will live. I do not want to go to a foster home. So many of the girls in here have been in and out of foster homes because of abuse and neglect. It is unfortunate to hear all of the different stories. I haven't really made friends with any of the girls yet, mostly because I do not trust them, and all they want to know is why I am in the CRH. I must tell so many grownups my story; I don't want to tell a bunch of girls too. I want friends because of who I am, not because of what I went through. Hopefully, if I am stuck here for a long time, I will make friends so I can stop feeling so lonely.

I am annoyed with myself that I miss my mom, I don't want to, but I do. I want her to get help so that I can have my family back. But, I am just not sure that is possible with how she continues to act, even while being off drugs for a bit. Maybe she can get the drugs in jail, and she will never get better, or perhaps it is not the drugs. It is just that she is evil.

Chapter 10

One Friday evening in mid-October, two FBI agents came to speak with me about Alexia's whereabouts. We are placed in an office. The two agents sit on one side of the desk facing towards the window that looks to the front desk. I sit in a gray office chair with my back to the window facing the agents. Both men seem large and intimidating. I was not sure why they need to talk to me. The agent's Jeff and Bill, spend a couple of hours breaking me down. At first, we went over the basics of what caused me to tell the police about my abuse. However, they would not let up about Alexia, flat-out telling me I was lying and that I knew what had happened to her. I kept up with the story that she is living with her father in Chicago, and they told me that Charles said he did not have her. I keep on with the story. That story is keeping me alive. If I told the truth and my mom was released, she would for sure kill me. I also did not want to hurt my Granny anymore; she was old and had heart issues. However, I could not kill her with the truth. They drilled me for most of that meeting, and I truly felt attacked.

Agent Rinek was not playing around; before I know it, he was using my feelings about my sister against me to break me down. It worked, too. Until that night, I had not cried once when telling my story or being moved to a receiving home. Agent Rinek was saying things as you cared for Alexia, and who do you think she was calling for when she was being killed? They kept saying that my sister was most likely dead and that I need to tell them what had happened. My mom was even blaming me, saying that I had killed Alexia. Nothing broke me, but he did by making me feel guilty about not doing more to give Alexia a proper chance to be found, dead or alive. I was sobbing so hard that CRH staff were trying to get in the locked room to get me out, even banging on the windows. After having enough, the last thing I said to the agents as I left the room was, "I don't give a rat's ass."

I left that meeting angry, hurt, and scared. The agents said horrible things to me. Them making me cry and trying to guilt me into sharing information was the worst. I hate crying, especially in front of others. I hate looking weak.

Chapter 11

The longer I am in the CRH, the more I hate it. All I want is to go live with my Granny. I do not understand why there are social workers and court dates that keep me from living with Granny. She is my only family. I do not know why they will not let me out. I feel like a prisoner sometimes. The CRH tries to make things suitable for all of us kids here, with field trips to places like the zoo parks, museums, seeing the Nutcracker, and such, but it is still different from the freedom of living with family. I also do not understand why I have to get visitors approved and have off-grounds lists and call lists. There are only two people I want to see and talk to my Granny and Mrs. Cooper. Why can't they just approve them and leave it be? I am tired of hearing it all takes time. The social workers are busy and need approval for my safety.

Most of the girls are moody and mean. I try to keep to myself, but that gets lonely too. I did make a friend, though. Her name is Dorothy. I trust her, and she helps me when I am upset. I will be happy for her when she gets to go home, but I will miss her when she leaves. That is another big reason I try not to make friends. People come and go daily here. I do not want to be hurt when they go. I love having off ground's visits. I get to break away and be free for a little while. I know I am lucky not many kids here have anyone or anywhere to go off-grounds. There are so many court dates for myself and my parents. I hate that I am not allowed to attend. If I get to go, I must wait in another room. I guess they do not want me in the court at the same time as my mom. I think that is good since I do not want to see her anyway. Now that I know how she feels about me and the lies she is saying about me, I genuinely hate her.

It's the day before Halloween, and dentists are here with their staff dressed in costumes. They talk about dental care and hand out candy. I am bored, but the little kids love it. Tomorrow, I have another court date. Hopefully, the judge will let me go live with Granny tomorrow. Halloween comes, and I get word they postponed my court date again; another hearing is set for November 10th. I am tired of being stuck here. I was informed that my mom's bail is set at one hundred thousand, and Larry does not get bail. As far as I know, no person will help my mom with bail, and she has no money. I am glad she is stuck. Granny calls me and tells me that Larry's family cleaned out the whole house. They took everything, even the hot tub. His family only left my waterbed and my mom's clothing. Granny hopes Larry's family will be accommodating and give back our things. I want my bike and rollerblades back.

I was not too fond of Halloween this year, and we could not even go real trick or treating. Not like I want to dress up and go trick or treating, but the little kids should be able to. Plus, this holiday makes me sad. Last Halloween, it was just Alexia and me when I took her around the neighborhood by Larry's house. I wish I could redo that night. I miss her more than one could imagine.

Chapter 12

It is the 2nd, and I am off the grounds; Mrs. Cooper came and got me and took me to my Granny's. We did not do much but hang out at her house, but I had fun anyway. I was also able to talk to my little brothers, they did not say much, but it was good to know they are happy and safe. Granny also shows me yesterday's newspaper. The headline read, "Elk Grove girl missing, feared dead." It was trippy to see, I did not read it, but I noticed there is a picture of Alexia by the headline. Granny wanted me to read it, but it just made me sad to think about it, and being off the grounds was supposed to be a fun break.

During the week, I had to meet with the police and detectives again. They make me take a lie detector test, and news flash, I lie. The police have obtained proof that I am lying. This information made them attack me harder for the truth. I finally broke down and told them the whole truth. First, the bleach milkshakes, Alexia's body in the freezer, then her being dismembered and burned. I gave them all the details they have been hounding me to provide. I think I shocked the detective, but he wanted the truth. Laura stays here with me and holds me. After a while, we all cry, sitting on the floor against the wall in the hallway. Having Laura by my side while retelling the horrible truth, I finally felt free and safe. My only worry right now is how Granny will take the news. I do not want to hurt her; she is all the family I have left.

This weekend I was able to have my first off-grounds weekend with Granny. I even got my hair done. It was needed because the bleach had ruined my hair. At least it is back to my natural color, and the lifeless hair was cut off. I feel much better now. Spending the weekend with Granny is terrific. We have to take the bus places since she does not have a car. We went to the mall to shop and get lunch. Granny made sure to have my favorite foods stocked up. She also recorded my shows so I could catch up. Another court date of mine has been postponed. I don't want to spend another month in this place. I am now considering a temporary foster home. I may upset Granny, but I no longer wish to be in the CRH. I want to return to a real school.

On the 7th, my mom's plea case was delayed, but she was found fit to stand trial. I cannot believe she tries to say she is not guilty but then says she is crazy. It does not matter to me if she is crazy or not. No one should be able to get away with what she did, just by saying they are insane. I do not understand how courts work, but none of this seems right to me. It feels like all we do here is wait for phone calls, visits, approvals, court dates, and field trips. I am, in reality, tired of waiting. I want to go home, to my home with my

Granny. Why is that so difficult to allow?

Chapter 13

Today is December first. My mom attends her plea hearing, and she pleads not guilty. I do not understand how she is authorized to plead not guilty; in her statement to the police, she admits to pouring bleach on me. The detective also tells me that they do not intend to charge my parents with the murder of my sister because of my instability. He said that I was not forthcoming about what happened to my sister. The jury is likely to believe that I am not a creditable witness. It is bullshit. I am the only witness, and what did they want me to do anyway. I was and am still terrified of being returned home to them.

What gruesome punishment would be dealt to me if I told the truth? I am still frightened that if they find her innocent and I have to go live with her again, I will be murdered, also. Things never end well for me when I speak up to my mom. Do they not understand that she is my mom and I must listen to what she instructs me to do? Even being away from her instability for the last couple of months, I believe I would still listen to her if she told me to do something. I just want her to love me and want me. I thought being a good girl would get me that. I was mistaken. My social worker says she does not believe I will be released this week due to media coverage of my case. I am not sure I believe her, but either way, I am stuck. Hopefully, I can get approval for an off-ground visit with my Granny for Christmas. I do not want to be stuck in the CRH on this holiday. To many heartbroken faces to deal with. Crying children that miss home and Santa is not the same in the receiving home.

The feelings I have about my mother and everything that happened in the past change often. Sometimes I hate her with all of me, and other times I wish she would get help and I could have a mom again. My mom always has a way of shattering my dreams. She has been writing my brothers and telling them that I am the one who killed Alexia and that when she gets out, she will get them and be a real mom to them. How can you write to a 6 and 4-year-old and tell them about a murder? Hopefully, their adoptive father did not show or read the letter to my siblings. Two months in jail and supposedly off drugs, and she still is mentally deranged. Things will never be okay.

It is Christmas, and I am spending it with my Granny. She went overboard with all of her gifts. In a way, she is trying to make up for what my mom did. I catch up on my shows, eat whatever I want, and just relax. I dread returning to the receiving home when I am off the grounds.

But I also miss my friends and staff there. I love my Granny; she does her best for me, but sometimes I am unsure if I want to live with her. I mean she is renting a room from Viola, and I would not have my own space, not even a bed. When I go for visits, I sleep on a single blow-up mattress on the floor beside Granny's bed. I will feel bad when I tell her I do not want to live with her because we are all each other has. Lately, she has been making me feel bad about my sister's death. I overheard her talking to Laura, the CRH social worker, when she came to pick me up. Granny was telling her if I had done things differently, if I had informed a neighbor or called a cop, anything, maybe I could have saved Alexia. I tried my best, and I honestly did, but I thought if I went to a neighbor and could escape the house, the words coming out of my mouth would make them think I was crazy. Granny does not understand how fear can freeze a person. I felt entrenched no matter the choices presented to me. Somewhere inside, I definitely wished things would improve, and I could have a mom who cared. I have enough personal guilt. I do not want to live with someone's blame too.

Chapter 14

I am back at the CRH, doing the same things every day, school, mealtime, craft time, and maybe some TV time. Nothing changes. I am at the point I do not think they are ever going to let me out of here. School is the only thing that keeps me going. I wish we were given homework so I would have something to do in the afternoons. School and chores only take up so much time. January sixteenth is a somber day. My best friend Dorothy and her brother got released. They will be in different foster homes but close to each other. I will miss her; I want to be happy for her, but I am jealous too. Maybe I will be lucky enough to see her off the grounds sometime soon. I officially asked my social worker Claudia to find me a foster home. I feel living with Granny full-time would be too much for both of us. My social worker pissed me off. She wants to put me in a group home; those are for bad kids and troublemakers. I told her no. I would rather stay at the CRH. I do not think I should be punished for my mom's crimes by having to go to a group home. I should be allowed to try a foster home before being forced into a group home. I am hopeful there is a family out there who might want to take a chance on me, right?

I want to talk to Dorothy, but I cannot because her foster parents have a 30-day no-contact rule, something about her settling into their home. I understand the rule, but what harm could a letter do? I am angry. I miss my best friend, and the girls admitted to the CRH after me are getting released. Why am I not wanted? Am I that bad of a person that no one wants me? The end of January is near, and I still have not heard from Dorothy. My Granny is upset with me because I do not want to live with her full-time. I have a couple of meetings with potential foster parents soon. Hopefully, I find one I like and that they feel the same.

Granny ended up in the hospital over the weekend. She was having problems breathing. Mrs. Cooper picked me up and took me to visit my Granny in the hospital. Granny looked unwell, but she still was flirting with all the doctors. Her not being well is another reason to look into foster homes. She has to be well enough to care for me, and I do not want to add any stress to her. Granny has always taken care of me, whether my mom was around or not. I would never want to be the reason something disastrous happened to her. She has been more of a mom to me than my mom ever will. I think it is time for her to be a grandma, to love and support me, but not to raise me. I do not feel heart surgery, and doctors' orders will get my Granny to change her ways. I try to get her to do as the doctors says and eat well, but she always says if I am going to die, I might as well die happy. I do not understand that, but I believe she should be happy.

Chapter 15

I chose a foster family, and they chose me. I thought moving into a stranger's home would be more challenging, but it was not. I was nervous the first day while meeting the whole family and learning the home's layout. I really thought I would be scared and unhappy. I guess coming from where I live. Through the hell I did, moving to a stranger's home, a walk in the park. The vibe in the house is so different from anywhere I have ever lived. I walked into kids laughing and dancing to kids' songs. The parents let me settle in on my own time, and I am getting a few days before I must start school. I have been in a real home for about a week. I am so excited tomorrow, 2-17-98, I am starting real school again. I am going to finish eighth grade at Center Middle school. I am very nervous about being a school again. Going to a new home is weird. I just showed up that day with my social worker.

I grabbed my black garbage bag that holds my things from the CRH. I had met the foster parents once before but not the rest of the family. The Saiters welcomed me into their home and gave me a place to feel safe. I had more freedom and, most importantly, a secure family. Including me, six kids are in the house ranging from 5 to 16 years old. We have chores and such, but we all work together to get things done. The foster mom makes sure to alternate Saturday errands with different kids, so we all get a chance at an outing and bonding time with her. I really missed family dinners and playing with the little kids. My foster sister Jessica is the same age as me, and we share a room.

I have to go by Lynn (my middle name). She is okay but loud and doesn't seem to follow the rules. It is my first day at Center Middle School, and I am lucky to have Mickey show me around. Starting a new school mid-year is tough. Trust me. I have done it a few times before. Things that first day are going well until 4th period, when the social studies teacher calls me in front of the class and asks me why I have not been in school the past few months. I tried to quietly tell her I was attending school in the receiving home. But, she repeated me loudly, and other students heard. My peers started teasing and laughing about me being in the receiving home. I was so embarrassed. It is terrible enough settling in a new home and school, but to have a teacher share my business sucked. After that, I get into the swing of school and even get to see Dorothy. She goes to high school next to the Middle School. We walk together to school each morning. I love being able to see my best friend every day. I do not think I have ever been this happy. I am ready for things to settle down. I need to get through whatever trial comes up for my parents so I can be happy in my new home. I even started calling my foster parent's mom and dad. I trust them.

Who would ever think that in not even two weeks, my happy life would be ruined again? I came home from school on the 25th. It was just a typical day. I walked in the door, ready for a snack and to start on my homework. I love doing my homework at the kitchen island, where mom can help as she gets snacks for the little kids. We get to chat about our day, and just have us time. Since most of the bigger kids like to run off to their rooms after school, it is just time for us, mom and I. Today is different. I walk into the house, and things feel off. I am immediately on edge. Then I see her Claudia, my social worker. I know something awful is about to happen. My social worker states she has to take me to the CRH for a meeting. I am on edge about what type of meeting and why does it have to be done at the receiving home. When we got to the CRH, Claudia informed me they had another status court date for me, and it was determined that at this point, I should not be in a foster home. I asked her what I did wrong, I am behaving, and school is going well. Apparently, the court determined I was not suitable for foster care at this time. I wanted a truthful answer. My rude attitude came out, and I yelled and cursed for the truth. They determined that I was potentially violent towards children, and I could not be in a home with young children anymore. I was crushed, but I did not cry. I just did as I was told. Later that night, my stuff appeared in a large black trash bag. My life, it seems, is very connected to black trash bags. I genuinely feel defeated for the first time, and three weeks of happiness ended.

Chapter 16

Claudia leaves, and I am alone. The only good thing about returning to the CRH is that I know how it is and what is expected of me. I walk past the front desk through the double metal doors, making my way down the brightly lit hallway, sneakers squeaking on the linoleum floor. I do not need an escort; I know the way to Willows I dorm. Walking into the dorm with none of my belongings is precisely like the first time I was brought here. The only difference is I have actual clothing on and not something that was given to me by the hospital. I am glad Barbara, my favorite staff is working this evening. She does not have to say anything, and even though the staff is not allowed to hug or touch us, she brings me in for a long hug. I needed it more than I thought. Her familiarity settles me a bit. She smells of mint gum and cigarette smoke. It's like coming home.

I got back into the CRH routine and made some new friends. Holly is fast becoming my best friend. She likes to care for me and can get me talking. She and her brother are here not due to abuse but due to her parent's drug use. The days are filled with more of the same, school, chores, and hanging out will Holly. Weeks go by, and I am without a social worker; they change so much. Not having a social worker is making things hard for me. They are the one who approves my call and visiting lists. I have just been outraged all the time.

I was happy in a foster home, and my whole world was disrupted. I have no outlet for my feelings, so being rude and hanging up on detectives and such when they call me makes me feel a bit better. Social services are trying to force me to go to therapy. I met with Sandy Baker several times, but I do not like therapy. She was trying to fit me in a box. All she kept asking is how do you feel about that? How the fuck does she think I feel? If I tell her something, she says I am depressed. I am not depressed; I am fucking angry. On my final visit with Sandy, I walk out, I am not sure I was allowed to do that, but I did. I made my way back to the dorms and left her sitting on the couch. I was so upset, and she just made it worse by telling me I was in denial and that the reason I cannot be in foster care was because of Larry and Barbara (I no longer call her mom, she does not deserve the title) said that I killed my little sister. I know they have said that before but if the courts will not allow me in a foster home, does that mean they believe it?

Since I am officially a ward of the court, I am allowed off the grounds by myself. We can earn the right to spend a couple of hours on our own, with good behavior and being responsible. Holly and I go out together. It is nice we walk to the convenience store near the CRH and get snacks that we cannot have at the home. The longer we behave, we can earn additional time on our own, but if we mess up, we can lose the privilege. Since I have been here, girls have yet to earn the honor of going off the grounds alone. I wonder if it is because they are irresponsible or have not been at the CRH long enough. Holly and I spend all of our time together. I have a major crush on her brother Mikey. He is cute. Not like he will ever know; we are not really allowed to hang out with the boys.

I met with the D.A. Marv Stern in the last week of March. He took me to lunch. He told me about the status of my parent's case, and we discussed my role when we go to trial. Marv said that Larry asked for a separate trial from Barbara because he thinks Barbara will put a spell on me. Larry is nuts. I finally have a new social worker, and her name is Laura. She met with my old social worker, my attorney, and Sandy, the horrible therapist. I wish these meetings included me since it is my life they are messing with. Laura told me she hopes to find me a foster home in April, but there can be no little kids or boys. I was confused about the boy part, and she said the therapist told her I had a boyfriend in my previous foster home. I do not know where Sandy gathered that information. See another reason not to do therapy? They lie. They also took Tami off my approved list for off-grounds visits, so now she can only visit during visiting hours. I do not understand why she was allowed to take me for outings before.

At the end of April, I spent the weekend at a potential foster home, but it was not the right fit for me. The foster mom was weird and too in my face. I would never be allowed any freedom with her. Holly gets released. I am happy she and her brother found a foster home together, but I am going to miss her. Holly left, giving me a best friend's necklace. She promised to always be my best friend. She was crying as she left, but I would not cry in front of her. I waited until she was gone. I then cried alone on my bed, hiding under my blanket. Everyone I love leaves me, and so many kids get foster homes. Why not me? I may not be getting a foster home any time soon, but I was appointed a CASA worker (Court Appointed Special Advocate). I always go into meeting people with the expectation of not liking them. So many people have hurt me, so I will not like you until I can trust you. I met with Judy and immediately got a good vibe from her. She told me about her life, her kids, and her family. We have the same taste in music and books. The point of the CASA worker is to get to know me by hanging out and doing fun things, and then she can report to the social workers what she thinks would be best for me based on truly knowing me. I hope we are able to do some fun things together. Going off the grounds again will be nice since Mrs. Tami is not allowed to take me anymore.

Holly's foster family did not work out, and she and her brother are back in the CRH. We both lost our off-grounds permissions, me for being rude, and Holly for being released. She has to earn it all over again. I do not generally have bad dreams, but last night I did. It was the worst. I dreamt that I was running through a forest and Barbara and Larry were chasing me. The worst part was when I looked back, and Alexia was chasing me too, but she was not normal. It was her, but she was all pieced back together. It was like a sewing job gone wrong. That dream was not how I wanted to enter a new month. I woke up on May 1st feeling all sick inside. What a way to start my birthday month.

Chapter 17

I am still not allowed to go off-grounds with Mrs. Tami, and I have not seen my Granny in a while. That sucks, but my CASA worker has been making it bearable, especially with Holly off the grounds most weekends. I am lonely without Holly, and I find it hard to sleep when she is gone. I have been spending a lot of time thinking about what my future will be like. I dream of having lots of kids. I think I will be a good mom and will not do any of the things my mom did. My most significant fear is that someone will take my children away from me. It scares me to think I may end up like Barbara. I would never want to be anything like her. She is pure evil. I am also scared that when I grow up, I will be alone. Who would want to love someone as broken as I am? I have been having a lot of sad thoughts, but I will not talk to anyone but Holly about them. Holly has a lot of the same fears as I do. But, I think if we work hard, we can make good lives for ourselves-one day.

The district attorney called me and said he thinks the trial will be some time at the end of June. I am scared to see my parents and tell a whole courtroom full of people what happened to Alexia and me. The D.A. said I would be on the stand for 2 to 3 hours, and both sides would question me. He also indicated that the defense would try to mess me up and upset me, so I get confused with my answers. I know I have to be strong and do what is right. I want Barbara to pay for how she hurt us. She was supposed to love and care for us, and she failed. She caused my sister's death, and her abuse of me is having lasting effects, not just emotional ones. I have to wear glasses now, and the doctor thinks that the bleach that Barbara put in my eyes could have caused my vision issues, especially since I have never had vision issues before. I despise wearing them, but I like being able to see.

It is May 15th, and it is my 14th birthday. Mrs. Tami came to visit me and brought me a new outfit. I talked to Granny on the phone. It was not the same as having a family gathering, but at least I got to talk to Granny. It's the day after my birthday and Judy my CASA worker took me to Marine World for the day. It was a blast, I loved seeing all of the animals, but it is like the zoo. It made me sad all of the animals are locked in cages.

Weeks go by. Nothing new happens. It is the same thing every day. I get to spend every Thursday with my Granny, have visits from Mrs. Tami, and get to go off the grounds with Judy. The rest of the time is just the same school, chores, and hanging out with Holly. I still have not earned my solo off-grounds back. I am furious about that. The trial date keeps getting postponed, and I am no closer to being released to a foster home. I feel like my life is at a standstill, and the entire world is moving on without me. I was looking forward to going off-grounds for the 4th of July, but I am not allowed. I feel like I am being punished for things I had no part of.

Chapter 18

In the CRH, any kid over thirteen can leave if they choose to. The staff cannot physically stop us from walking out the front doors or jumping a fence. With not being allowed any off-ground visits with Mrs. Tami or overnights with Granny, I feel like I am being held captive. My social worker told me she could not approve any visits without the approval of my lawyer and the bitch of a therapist Sandy (my words, not hers), because my case is such a high profile. I was pissed. I do not care about the media and my case status; I want an average teen life. I asked her what would happen if I went AWOL for the holiday. She said it was my decision and that she would not punish me for doing it. I took the time to think about all of the possible consequences, including losing my spot in the CRH if another kid needed the bed; it was worth the risk to me. Holly and I worked out a plan that I would go AWOL 4th of July weekend. I was so excited to hang out with my best friend and crush without tons of staff around, running all of our fun.

That Friday evening, I worked up the nerve to walk out the front door. I packed a small bag with some clothes and my makeup. Three minutes to 8 pm, I told the staff, Sandy, that I was leaving. She said no, you're not. As I walked out of the dorm, I heard Sandy call the front desk to let them know I was coming. I walk up the long hallway, and as I was about to pass the front desk to leave, I was stopped by Dee and Sharon, who was telling me about the dangers of leaving. I was even made to write down what I was wearing. Then, I received a phone call; it was Mrs. Tami. I took the call as the staff at the desk listened and watched me. Mrs. Tami knew my plan; I am unsure if she genuinely thought I would do it.

I ended the call, and the staff tried to convince me to stay. I said no and that I would be back Sunday evening. I just walked out the door and down the road to Dairy Queen, where Holly and her dad were waiting for me. Holly told her dad I was coming from my grandma's house.

That night we went to many of Holly's friend's houses. We ended up staying at Jaime's house, where we got high. In the morning, we were walking to Holly's grandma's house. Along the way, her grandma picked us up, and we went to the store where Holly got smokes with my two dollars. After some back-and-forth hanging out at her grandma's, we ended up at her uncle's house. We had a barbecue and waited for it to get dark to light fireworks. Amber and I helped Holly's little sister with fireworks while the boys were being stupid with the fireworks and talking about getting head. They were a wild mess. I just laughed at them all. We returned to her uncle's house and watched the

Howard Stern Movie when the night was over. Then we slept the night away on the floor. With 12 teenagers, there was no room on the couches. Sunday came, and we all went to Water World. I was surprised they let me in wearing shorts and a t-shirt. It was a long day in the sun going down the lazy river, breaker beach, calypso cooler, and all the slides. I had so much fun. I had never been to water world before. My mom would never take me to do something like that. She always said you cannot do it if I have to drive, or it costs money. We finished the evening at Holly's uncles until her parents came to get me. Around 11 pm, they did and dropped me off at the Science Center on the same road as the receiving home.

I walked back to the CRH and walked in, and the woman who did my intake was at the front desk. I gave her my name, and she began to give me a lecture about how unsafe it was that I ran away and it was a bad thing to do. I told her I knew all that before leaving and chose to go anyway. As she could see, I was back and fine. I was tired and cranky, so she just pissed me off. She handed me a questionnaire about my time away. It said where did you go? What did you do? Who were you with? I answered I went with friends. To water world and fireworks, and I had to leave to stay sane. The front desk lady tried to get more information about who I was with, but I just shut up. She did not need to know my business. All she should be concerned with is that I am back and need a bed. I took a nice shower and went to bed.

In the morning, Denise came to me with my restriction paperwork and asked how was your weekend with Holly? I told her to fuck off. In the few days following my AWOL, I receive a lot of lectures on how bad and unsafe it was for me to run away. I am angry about it all. I know for sure only two people genuinely give a damn about my safety and well-being. The rest are worried about the liabilities if something had happened to me on their watch. Most of the time in the receiving home, I feel like just a number or just a face in a large group. I am sure some of the staff care about us kids personally. The rest is more concerned about a paycheck and keeping the kids safe. The kids being happy and feeling wanted are not a part of being safe and cared for. Besides getting a mental break by running away, my social worker finally seems more on my side. She is trying to get the team of people who decide my life to loosen up on some of the restrictions so she can actually find me a foster home. I am not sure what to think about that. Maybe I should have run away sooner since following the rules has not gotten me far.

Chapter 19

Holly was released to a foster home a couple of days after our fun weekend. I miss her so much, and I am not sure how to handle being stuck here without her. I attempt to focus on school. I keep to myself even though it is a lonely existence. I am working on my friendship bracelets. Creating beautiful designs in my embroidered bracelets keeps my mind busy. I am searching for any way to keep my thoughts off missing Holly. I hope Holly will call me soon. This week has been miserable. Soon, Laura is having her last day. She is the CRH social worker, and she helps us all tremendously. I am going to miss her and her loud laugh. All the people I need are leaving me or are being taken away. I do not think anyone understands how I feel being one of the teenagers in the CRH longer than any other child. I feel so broken and unwanted. I do not know what else I can do for someone to believe in me and want me. Maybe all the things Barbara told me are true: I am unlovable and a horrible waste of life. If my own mom feels that way about me, it must be easy for others to feel the same way.

With Holly in a foster home, I feel alone. I do not have my person who helps me with everything. I am sad and angry, which makes me grumpy and irritable. The grumpier I am, the more I have an attitude. There have been a bunch of new girls in the dorm too. We are all vastly different, and a few like to start shit with other girls. One new girl is telling everyone I am a bitch. Well, I am to her for sure. I am tired of all our dorm meetings, demanding everyone to play nice. At least we had each other when Holly was here. We could vent our issues to each other. I hope I get released soon. Being here is getting very hard to handle. I want to work on my attitude, but I see no point when I am not treated fairly. It is coming to the end of July, and I hope to go to a foster home in the summer. I want to have some time to get to know my new foster parents, and learn the rules of the house before school starts. I will be starting high school in yet another school. Making new friends and trying to fit in is hard enough without being thrown into a new home.

It is August 22. Judy took me to get my hair done, and then we went to the state fair. Since I knew we were going, I planned to meet Holly, Mike, and Meghan there. I did not tell Judy my plans, and she was upset that all my friends were there. I did not care because it had been almost two months since I had a chance to hang out with my Holly. I had so much fun being able to be myself. I did not have to worry about rules, chores, trails, social workers, or anything but having fun with my best friend. I was able to feel like a typical teen for a few hours, not someone's burden. We ate fair foods, watched a hypnotist show, and rode many rides. By the night's end, my feet hurt, my face was sunburnt, and my cheeks were sore from laughing so much. Holly wouldn't go on any of the upside-down rides with me, but Mikey did, and being so close to him to did not help my crush at all. I cherish these rare days that I get to be an average teen.

Chapter 20

The last weekend in August, and I am spending a weekend at a foster home for a pre-placement. If I like it, I can stay. I don't particularly appreciate that it is far from Sacramento, where my Granny and friends reside. Over an hour's drive for visits will not be easy. Granny has no car, so I am unsure how I will get to see her. The town is so small, and there is nothing to do. The foster parents, David and Rosie, seem likable, but I am sure they all do in the beginning. The family is too religious for me. I will not attend church; they go 3 to 4 times weekly. They said they would not make me attend church, but I could not stay home alone. Shit, I am 14 and cannot stay home alone for a couple of hours. So, what am I going to do? Run away, shit into the miles of woods that surround the home. Come on now. So if I do not attend church, I must go to a babysitter or wait inside the church while they have service. My only condition is that I am able to see Holly, Tami, and my Granny somehow. The social worker said she will make it so I can spend time with Holly, so I guess I will stay.

I share a room with their teenage daughter Melanie. She is my age and is a skinny cheerleader type. Stuck-up and boy-crazy, just the kind of girl I hate. The room is just big enough for her full-size bed and my twin bed. She is boy-crazy and worried about her boyfriends and makeup over anything else. She is in love with every boy and cries so much over them. I do not think that girl has ever known real pain. I get signed up for school and start my freshman year at Paradise High. It takes a couple of weeks, but I get a routine down and make good grades. School is all I have for me to keep busy. I haven't made any friends because I do not want to. I do not see myself staying in this foster home long term. I guess it is just a feeling I have about this situation.

I look forward to my weekly calls with Mrs. Tami. I call her collect from the school's pay phone. It is nice to talk to her. I miss her and do not understand why I am not allowed to see her or talk on the phone. I guess I will have to keep sneaking calls until the social worker allows me contact with her. I am trying my best to be a good kid and student so that I am permitted to have visits and such. It is unfair to me how things are so different for the actual children of the foster parents. There is so much more freedom and happiness. I cry myself to sleep each night and always have headaches. This is my life now, and I have no clue how to improve it.

Halloween comes, and once again, we are at the Cruz's church. I do not get why they go to church so much. What is God going to do for them? The foster parents preach significantly about religion and saving your virtue, but their daughter is a major slut. Why doesn't Jesus get her to keep her legs closed? While they constantly preach to me, I haven't even had a real first kiss yet. Well, anyway, I go to the church with them to volunteer at the Jamboree. I am helping at the race car game. I enjoy playing with the little kids and seeing them all dressed up. They are so sweet and have so much fun. Their smiles and laughter almost make me truly happy too. I think it is so messed up that I was taken from my first foster home because of my potential to be violent towards little kids, but at this foster home, I can live with a seven-year-old boy, babysit at the church, and help kids at the Jamboree. Why is it okay now? What changed in the last eight months? The system is a mess; the people who genuinely care and want to do what is best for the kids cannot due to all the rules and regulations.

November comes, and I find out I cannot have overnight visits with Holly. I am required to have supervised visits with my Granny. I am so angry. I do not have many people in my life that I love and trust, and the system is taking them all away. They only want me to do as I am told and see another counselor. I have seen her several times, but I do not talk. I tell her she is wasting both of our time. I feel talking with the people I trust is better therapy for me. I do not understand why the social workers keep pushing the issue. November 3, and I have to go to Sacramento but not for the reason I want. I must meet with the D.A. to tape my testimony and review things before the trial. He thinks it will be postponed again until sometime in 1999. It was an unbelievably hard day for me. I had to relieve everything and tell it on camera. I broke down a couple of times but not on camera. I do not want them to have my breakdown recorded. I was so upset because I still love my mom and would like to be with her again if she got help. I do not know how to stop loving her. I know I should because of what she did, but I just cannot. Even knowing she hates me and wants me to die, I still want to be with her. I am angry at this whole situation and that I am being forced to testify against her. I am starting to hate myself because I am so torn. I want a mom; I want my mom. This is never going to get any easier.

The highlight of the day is that Laura came to support me during the interview, and we were able to go to lunch to gather. I miss seeing her daily, like when she worked at the CRH. It was a very long day, and I had to tell them why I lied about what happened to my sister. Marv says that is going to be used against us in the trial. I would say I am sorry for lying, but I am not. I was doing as I was told, being a good girl for my mom. I wanted to protect her. Despite all the twisted shit she had done to me and my siblings, she is still my mom and always will be. Being back in Sacramento, even just for the day, close to all of my support people, makes me more sure that I do not want to live in Magalia with the Cruz's.

On the 2nd Saturday in November, I finally saw my Holly. We had to go to Sacramento for my foster brother's pass, punt, and kick event. So my foster parents were dropping me off with Holly at her grandma's house. I was supposed to stay with her until six pm, but they came and got me early because I had to have dinner with my foster parent's parents. I did not want to go or need to meet them, but I had no choice. I never have a choice. My whole life comprises other people's choices, good, bad, and in between. I was trying to be happy and grateful for the few hours I was able to spend with Holly. On the long drive back up to Magalia, I was talking about my visit and how Holly was my Holly. Then Rosie was like we are the ones who brought you to see Holly. I was confused, but I said I know that, and thank you. She explained more about how they made the trip to bring me for this visit, like what I should bow to their feet. I got angry and said, it is not like you genuinely went out of your way to bring me to see Holly. You were coming to Sacramento anyway for your son's football thing. Do not try to make it like it was all about me. Nothing in this home is about me.

I spend my nights crying, and they know I do. I must go to the D.A. and relive hell, but neither checks on me. When I came home from my day of recorded testimony, no one asked me how it went or how I was feeling. They ignored me as a whole. I hate living with them. The receiving home was better. At least the staff cared and wanted to be there for me. I hate feeling so stuck and having no way to call my people. David does not like to let me use the phone because it is long distance.

Chapter 21

November 21, 1998, I was moved to my third foster home. This home is in Marysville and much closer to Sacramento, still about 45 minutes away, but this will allow me to visit people more easily. The house is at the end of a cul-de-sac. It is large seven bedrooms, with a pool and basketball court. The family is the Perrys, Donna and David. They are an older couple with grown kids, but they are incredibly nice. Their son Rob lives in the house with his wife Lynn and their 20-month-old daughter. Johanna was a foster kid, but the Perry's took guardianship of her. She has her own room. During the first couple weeks, I am just settling in at my new home and high school. I have made some friends at school but do not want to see them outside of school. I try to limit my time with other people at school. I am not a social butterfly. I, most of the time, dislike people. The Perry's give us 100 dollars a month, and we can use it for anything, but we have to buy our toiletries with it. Dave says he does it this way so that we can learn to budget. I like it because I have money for fun stuff too. I am actually happy and feel loved in this home. Dave allows me more freedom, even going against my social workers' rules. She said no overnight visits with Holly, but Dave worked it out with her foster parents, and we have had three visits in the first month I lived here. Dave and Donna break the rules a bit because they want us girls to be able to have a normal life as a teen. They see themselves as our parents and believe they should be able to make those choices because they know us. As long as we are responsible and respectful, we get more options than I have seen in my other placements.

The Perrys make me feel wanted and valued. I love that they are so willing to help me be able to see my friends, Granny and Mrs. Tami. There is some drama when new girls come into the home, but Dave and Donna have a way of smoothing it out without yelling or punishment. I hope I can stay with them until I am 18. Mike and I officially became boyfriend and girlfriend on 12-9. Dave is not really happy about me dating, but he trusts me to be safe no matter what choices I make. I am only allowed supervised visits with Granny. I do not understand why. She has always been good to me. I will not ever understand all the different rules and regulations in the foster care system. I should just be happy I am allowed to see her, even though it is not the same. I was allowed to see Granny for a Christmas visit at Environmental Alternatives (a foster care program), supervised, of course. Granny and I exchanged presents, and she brought me homemade cookies. I love her cookies. I want more time with her, and an hour's visit is just not long enough. Plus, Granny needs to be in better health, and the travel cannot be that good for her.

Mike and Holly's school plays against my school. He is on the basketball team. So, Holly came to my house, and we went to my school to watch the game. I know nothing about basketball and dislike sports, but I went anyway. Anyway, going to the game turned out to be the best night of my life. I had my first kiss. I was so nervous, and too many people were around, but it happened. After that, things are good, and I have a routine that allows many visits with Holly. Things are going so well that the Perry's want to take legal guardianship of me, and for the first time ever, it seems my social worker, the lawyer, and all others in charge think it is a good idea. So, we have a court date in early June to see if the judge will approve their request to apply for guardianship. If they get approved, we will no longer have to follow the system's rules, and they will be my legal parents.

May is here, and I will be fifteen this month. I am looking forward to my birthday this year. The Perry's are going to Idaho to see David's mom for a long weekend. I get to go and miss a couple of days of school. I am so excited about this trip. I have never been to Idaho. We get to Reno, and Dave gets word that I cannot go to Idaho. My social worker was not able to get the approval for me to go out of state. What B.S. why are things so hard? We were trying to take a family trip. So, Rob had to come to get me and drive us back to California. I was hurt and felt terrible the trip was delayed, and Rob had to go out of his way to bring me back home. Mrs. Tami and I had a visit on the 13th, and she brought me money from the account she set up for me. I was able to get my pager. I chose a teal one. I am glad that my family and friends will be able to reach me now.

My 15th birthday was a blast, and Lynn made it so special. I was surprised with Holly and a trip to San Francisco. We shopped at all the little shops on the pier, played in the arcade, rode the carousel, and had dinner at a Chinese restaurant. It was so much fun to hang out, and Caitlyn enjoyed the arcade. That is a big deal when you are two. We returned home on the 15th, my birthday, and had cake with the rest of the family and lots of swimming. It was the best birthday I can ever remember. I got to see all my favorite people and do fun things. The only thing that would have made it better was to have a visit with Granny.

I finish freshman year, looking forward to a fun and happy summer. It has been a long time since I enjoyed summer. The Perrys are enrolling me into charter school on July 1. I am super excited because I hate going to school. All the kids and drama are too much for me. With charter school, I can graduate early. I really would like to graduate early so I can start college early. I am torn between wanting to be a lawyer or a social worker. I want to make a difference for kids like me. Summer is full of visits with Holly and Mike. Lynn and Rob took Holly and I to a church festival concert thing. It was a long weekend away, staying in an RV. It was so much fun. I am not into church and God, but the trip was a fun way to see Holly and meet new people. Holly and I talked about what we want our futures to be. We both want to get married, have many babies, and hopefully be sisters by marriage (ha-ha). We do not want to be like our parents or drug addicts. Her parents lost them because of drug abuse. So, we have plans to finish high school, not have any babies before college, and stay away from drugs. Hopefully, we can do it with hard work and have a better life than our parents.

The summer is full of fun and many firsts for myself. On my weekends to see Holly, I drank alcohol and got high.

I am trying out different things. I like to have a couple of beers, but getting high is not my favorite. I get a bit paranoid and feel like I cannot breathe. Telling myself to breathe on repeat is not my idea of a good time. I also lost my virginity to Mike that 4th of July weekend. Telling Mrs. Tami about it and asking for help getting birth control seemed almost too much for her. What did she think? I would stay a virgin forever. Not likely. She picked me up one day, and we drove around Sacramento to find a Planned Parenthood so I could get birth control. We ended up in the wrong location. Going into the building there were so many guards. We were both confused until we went to the check-in window, and they told us we were at the abortion clinic. That explained the guards. We both were a bit scared and humiliated being at the wrong place. Finally, we found the correct type of clinic in a town close to my foster home, and I was set up with birth control and a bag full of condoms. It was an adventure that I was glad to have had with Mrs. Tami. Anyone else would not have been as supportive or helpful.

The summer ends, and so does my idyllic life. The Perrys are moving, and the judge decided against allowing them to take guardianship of me. I am not sure what happened, but I guess it was because they allowed so much time with Holly and Mike without permission from the social workers, and they did not want to allow me to move out of state. The courts want to keep me around so I can be readily available for the trial. I am the key witness, and I have to testify. It is another way my mom and Larry are screwing up my life. I thought getting away from them would stop their interference. I was so wrong. I am devastated and scared to have to go to another foster home. I want to be eighteen, so I can have some control over my life. I do not know what it is about me that people feel like I do not deserve happiness. I am good. I get good grades. I don't run away, and I am not pregnant. Sometimes I genuinely wonder what the point of being responsible is. I see other foster girls/teens who have babies and are dropping out of school get more freedom and choices than I do. I just keep thinking, what the fuck will be next.

Chapter 22

It is September of 1999, and my guardianship with the Perry's was not approved. I thought I would be moving into a new foster home, but it turned out my new foster mom Joan Clearwater is coming to me. She is renting the Perry's house for a time. It is wonderful that my environment does not have to change when everything else is. Joan is a fun lady, such a hippie. Long gray hair, smokes a lot and has this let live and let be vibe. I hope that works in my favor. She brought her two foster daughters with her. They are a couple of years younger than me. Joan is going to let me keep attending the charter school. It will work well for the other girls as well. Only having to go to class once a week is so enjoyable. I find it funny that they would not let me stay with the Perrys because they broke some of the social worker's rules, but Joan doesn't seem to know what a rule is. We stayed in the house in Marysville for a couple of months. After the new year, we moved to Joan's home in Loma Rica.

I thought I would hate living there since it is so far from any town and nothing but land around the tiny home. The house is so small it did not even have a bedroom. Joan built a wall to create a room. Two girls stay in that room, Joan has a converted construction trailer on the land for her room, and I stay in Joan's R.V. I was initially unsure about living in the R.V. because it was not a real home, but I quickly learned I loved having my own space and bathroom. It may be small, but I enjoy the freedom as the oldest. I become super close with Joan, I never entirely put her in the mom role and always called her Joan, but she got me. I think she was lonely, and the foster girls were her friends more than anything. I was okay with that because I was responsible and did not need much "parenting." Joan allows me to keep having my weekends with Holly and Mike. She would take me to town on a Friday, and I would take the bus down to Sacramento. I caught the bus back on a Sunday, and Joan would be waiting for me to take me home. She was fine with whatever I wanted as long as I kept up with my classwork, did some chores around the house, and stayed on my birth control. I was living my best life, and I never wanted to give up my freedom. It was all teens' dream life; she even let us drink with her sometimes by the fire pit. I could see why the legal powers at hand would not like that and the liabilities it could bring.

Chapter 23

The new year brought many changes, good, bad, and indifferent. My parent's trial was finally happening. On February 10th, my mom pleads guilty to the second-degree homicide of my 5-year-old little sister. This same day the jury selection occurred for my stepdad Larry's trial. I am nervous. This is all so real now. My testimony and facing them had been far-off over the past couple of years. With each lawyer change, plea change, and other delay tactics by the defense, I was able to allow myself to believe the hearing would never happen. I would not have to face them. I wanted to get the trials over with so they could be sentenced, and I could have some closure and move on, but the realism of it all was very difficult to process. Maybe a part of me was trying to wish it all away, and the more time passed, the more I could pretend to be an ordinary, not broken girl. Over the past two years, I have spent a lot of time daydreaming and allowing my mind to give me a whole different life. This trial bursts that bubble in a big way. Time to put my emotional wall back up. It is the only way I know how to be present and be able to tell the tale of my abuse. I have to narrate it all like it is a story I read or a movie I saw. I have no emotive reactions when I tell of the horrors I lived through. I do not know if it is a good healthy way to process things, but it has worked for me during the abuse, and now reliving it.

The jury selection for Larry is completed. On Valentine's Day, I must face him. He pleads not guilty to all charges forcing me, the only witness, to testify. I want to sit in and participate in the trial, but I am not allowed to. The waiting to testify is tough. The longer I have to wait, the more anxious I become. I am scared that when I see his face and hear him speak, I will freeze and be unable to speak against him. I do not want to allow him to have that kind of control over me, but I am fearful of it. So many people are counting on me, and I might just let them all down. I have been told there is not much of a case without my testimony, and even that may not be enough because there are no remains, and I did lie in the beginning. I have to suck up my fear and do this for Alexia, I was not able to get past my fear to take action to save her life, but I must get past my fears to give her justice.

I am finally brought into the courtroom, made to sit in front of a courtroom full of people. I am trying to avoid looking at Larry. I will only focus on the D.A. I swear to tell the truth, and the questioning begins. Marv is asking me to recount in detail what happened in the summer of 1996. It is hard because I can feel Larry looking at me, his angry stare is burning into my body. For the most part, Larry looks uninteresting in being there, but I caught a few grimaces on his face when I went into detail on his part of Alexia's murder. I do not mind answering Marv. We have spent many lunches and meetings together reviewing my testimony. With him, I feel like he believes in me and wants to support me no matter the outcome.

Larry's defense attorney has his turn to question me, and all I keep thinking about is the fact that he looks like the scientist from the movie Back to the Future. He asks many of the same questions as the prosecution, but he is trying to get me to change my answers. He is a dick. I was informed prior to the trial that he might be mean in order to get me to act out. He was trying to make me look like an incompetent witness. At one point, he asked me when an event occurred, and I first said during the week, and at another point, it could be the weekend. He was a bit loud and, in my face, "well, which is it, the week or weekend? I answered that I was not sure because I was locked in that house all summer. The days just ran together when I was trying to survive. Hours of testimony later, I was finally done. The trial was three days long. Ultimately, Larry was found guilty of second-degree murder and ten counts of child abuse and torture. The following month on March 17th, 2000, Larry was sentenced to 40 years to life.

After the trial, life goes back to normal. I am still living with Joan and my foster sisters in Loma Rica, attending the charter school and visiting Holly and Mike on most weekends. I was happy, safe, and working towards my goal of early graduation. Joan was also working on trying to get guardianship of me. I thought this place is where I would stay until I was eighteen, maybe a chance at a real mom. Although Joan was more of a friend than mom, she let me do what I wanted and would party with us kids too. My teen self was living in bliss. I turned sixteen that May, but it was bittersweet. I could not learn to drive because the system will not allow it since the state would not want to be responsible if I were to get into an accident. Being a foster kid blows. We cannot do many things, but the foster parent's natural children can. I am hopeful if Joan can get guardianship, I will be able to learn to drive and get a car.

On May 23rd, my mother is found sane to stand trial. Currently, she decides to take a plea deal. She pleads guilty to second-degree murder, and they dropped all the child abuse charges. Not having to testify in another trial is wonderful to me, because I know facing her would be worse than facing Larry. I am glad they will be imprisoned for the murder and my little sister gets her justice, but in the legal world, it is like my abuse did not happen. Either way, I know she is going to prison, but I want her to take responsibility for what she did to us. On June 20th, Barbara was sentenced to 15 years to life. I attend her sentencing with Joan, Mrs.

Tami, and my former CRH social worker Laura. I was offered a chance to speak at the hearing but could not. I felt no matter what I said, she would turn it around. I did not want to give her any satisfaction in knowing how her actions and abuse hurt me. When Barbara was brought out to the courtroom, she did glance back at me. I made a point to stare her down each time she tried to peek at me. I wanted to be strong, and staring silently was the only way I knew I could accomplish that. Even three years later, I feared Barbara's hold on me and the little girl inside who just wanted her mom to love her.

Chapter 24

I thought life would remain the same and I could finally be emotionally free after all of the trial stuff was finished. I wanted to focus on school and just being a teen. Joan was denied guardianship of me because somehow they found out she let us kids drink with her. I was so angry at being denied another chance at a real permanent home. Joan also lost her foster care license, and all three of her foster girls had to be placed in new foster homes. Things were the most unstable for me at this time. I was moved to two different foster homes staying at each one for a couple of weeks. The fifth was to removed from town. The mother was mean and strict. She was almost militant. Her biological teen daughter hated her and lived in the guest house just to be away from her. We both were unhappy with the placement, and she asked that I be moved to another home, and I agreed. At the sixth foster home, they locked the fridge and food away, only allowing us to eat what they made, and on my first day there, after a few hours, they left. The foster parents had plans and left. The other foster teen stays long enough to show me how to use the television, and then she took her baby and left too. I was shocked being all alone on the first day. I stayed in my room, refusing to unpack my trash bag of things. The first chance I had, I asked to be moved to another home.

I moved in around the end of August. I was the oldest of all the foster kids. I learned quickly that I was to be the caretaker of other kids. The home was in Brownsville, a small town with few dwellings around. There were three other foster kids, and they had a toddler that was their child. The first weekend I was there, I had her baby strapped to my chest, walking with the other kids a mile or so down the road to the local convenience store. There were no toys or anything to keep us kids entertained. The foster dad worked as a teacher in Sacramento, so he had over an hour commute each way. The mother, I believe, was from Russia and had a completely different way of parenting. There was no television either, and keeping us entertained for the remainder of summer was extremely hard. I was heartbroken not being able to see Holly and Mike and having to go back to regular high school. I was not too fond of traditional school. I was never good at fitting in am making friends. Truly after so many moves, there was no point in finding friends and happiness because it could be taken from me so quickly.

I was forced to return to Marysville High School and kept to myself. I was in a very dark place. I maintained good grades but shied away from my high school experiences. I was lost again, trying to figure out how to get by in this new place living a life I hated. When I was not at school, I was a babysitter, making dinner helping with homework, and so forth. If I wanted to parent, I would have had my own baby. Instead, the foster mother lived in her own world and was easily distracted. That is why caring for the little kids became my job. It was easier and safer to do it myself. I was unhappy and frustrated with how this home worked, so I kept a journal of every time I was left alone or had to care for the kids.

The neglect was apparent, we were not abused in the home, but none of us were thriving either. She left us once at a local pool. She paid to get in gave me a 20-dollar bill for snacks and left us for hours. I had no way to contact her if something happened. I was anxiety-ridden that one of the little kids would drown, and another death would be my fault. Another time she left the dog locked in her car, and it died from the heat. The social worker, at first, did not want to hear what I had to say. She kept telling me I was looking for reasons to go to another home, because I wanted to go back with Joan. It was weeks of arguing with the worker and getting nowhere.

We had a half day at school, and I took the opportunity to sneak a visit with Joan. She got me from the school and took me to the other school near my foster home to get on that bus. The elementary school had a full day, so I was able to sneak in a couple of hours with her. I missed her, and she seemed so sad and lonely now. The bus driver told me I could not change pick-up stops like that, but I never got in trouble for it, and I do not think my foster parents found out. I do not believe she would care anyway. The final straw in my 7th placement that convinced the social worker to believe me, was when she came for a visit, and all 4 of us foster kids were sitting outside the house in the heat after the bus dropped us off. It was a least an hour after the bus dropped us off. The social worker showed up, and neither foster parent was there, and we needed access to get into the home. The worker waited another hour with us until our foster mom showed up. This social worker was not my personal worker but one for the foster agency that certified the home. She took my notes and believed me. I was relieved to have someone listen and want to help.

Chapter 25

It is October of 2000 I have been moved to another foster home. I was moved from the Brownsville home with two little girls. They will only stay in this foster home for a few weeks until their adoption is final. Going into this move, I feel defeated. I do not want to like the people or the home because all the good things and people in my life get taken away. It is hard to keep fighting when no one wants me. I give myself a pep talk to be strong and keep progressing towards my goals but always be ready for another heartbreak. Good things are always taken from me. I need to be prepared so I won't fall apart when it happens. I dream of a certain future and cannot let my emotions dictate my actions. It is best for me just to be angry. Being angry keeps a lot of the hurt away.

The three of us are taken to Yuba City to our new home with the Hurds. The girls hold my hand and stay beside me while inductions are made. I try to smile and be excited about a new home to ease their fears. They both cling to my side as we are shown around the house and our rooms. I am so happy these two little girls will be getting a forever home. I always wondered if I would meet any family that would love and want me enough to adopt me. Not likely older kids are often overlooked for adoption because we are not tiny and cute, and most have tons of emotional baggage. I was labeled a problem child in the eyes of the system, not by my actions but by those of my parents. I think it would have been easier to be the child they made me out to be, with less work and disappointment. It always feels like I am never enough, so I keep working on my goals but with a major attitude and anger toward everyone around me.

The Hurds are a large family, JR and Dawn, who both had two kids from previous relationships and then married and had a son. The house is full of teens. They seem friendly, but the teens are more of the popular type. That is not me. I keep to myself a lot. I am grateful that they allow me to return to the charter school. Hopefully, I will still be on track to graduate early. I settle into a routine but keep my guard up. I sometimes think I am broken like I cannot get attached to people anymore. So many moves and changes in the last three years have damaged parts of me. I wonder if I will ever be able to put them back together. The rules of the foster care system that are there to keep kids safe also hinder us from finding our full potential. The rules are based on a whole demographic, not based on each child. I wish there were a way to allow the foster parents more decision-making power since they know the child best.

A few weeks into living with the Hurds, I was able to contact Mrs. Tami. The social workers banned her from seeing or talking to me. I got permission to call her from Dawn. I wanted to check on my Granny too. I know she had not been well. The system did not want me to have contact with Granny either. I never got an honest answer as to why I had such limited contact with the only true family I have. When I finally could talk with Mrs. Tami, she gave me the worst news ever. My Granny had passed. No one told me my only family member was gone, and there was no service for her. I was confused about how Mrs. Tami knew. I asked who called her and not me. She told me that no one had called her. It was a tragedy that brought her to the person who told her. On October 3rd, a former classmate of mine from Mrs. Tami's math class committed suicide. Mrs. Tami went to the service for Jenny. Another student I used to write to told Mrs. Tami that my Granny had passed. Apparently, my Granny's boyfriend had her things, including some of my mail. He wrote to the girl, letting her know so she could contact me if she knew where I was. It is awful to learn of a family member's death alone but to have another tragedy bring it full circle.

I got off the phone and cried for the first time in a very long time. I thought I would never stop. Dawn and Big Jen came into my little room and comforted me. There were hugs and sweet words and the breaker of the sad is when Jen pulled her sweatshirt over her head and started talking like Beavis and Butt-head. That moment broke the tension, and it was the moment I knew I had found a family. I wanted to stay and have parents and siblings. It was a hard feeling to embrace, and I kept the attitude. I always wondered if the system knew my Granny had passed and chose not to tell me.

I continued charter school and began working full-time babysitting a two-year-old boy named Harrison and his older sister when she got out of school. This job was perfect for me as I could do my schoolwork while earning money. Months pass I am able to graduate a year and a half early. I completed high school in January 2001. That same month I started my first semester at Yuba College. Although, it was odd being a 16-year-old in college, I got used to it really quick. College is much better than high school, with less drama and more people focused on their studies. I guess paying for classes makes one want to do their best. Focusing on school, I have had less time to talk to Holly and Mike. I miss them both.

Chapter 26

I, along with the other foster kids, are enrolled in a foster care program put on at the college. It is called ILP, Independent Living Program. It is put on to teach foster kids skills for living on our own. We meet at the college each Wednesday evening for food and a lesson. We are taught skills like how to make a resume and balance our checkbooks. I enjoy attending this class because it is filled with lost kids like me. The program is run by county social workers and professors at the community college. Besides the weekly classes, we were taken on multiple trips, some for fun and others for learning. We went on one trip to a Sacramento Hotel, staying overnight. During the day, we spent the day learning computer programs, PowerPoint and excel. After completion of the training, each participant was sent home with a new computer and printer.

While getting a computer was fabulous for college classes. The most fun I had that weekend was after lock-in when we were restricted to our hotel room. I was with two other teen girls, and we were lucky that we had no adult supervision in our room. The room had a small kitchenette, so I went through the cabinets and hit gold. There I found a half-full bottle of Crown Royal. A couple of boys on the trip snuck over to hang out with the other girls, and we all got a buzz from that bottle. I was made fun of because I did not invite any boy over. I was too committed to Mike that the thought of another guy was gross. Males were friends only. As far as I know, the staff never knew the trouble we were up to that weekend. I thoroughly enjoyed doing something so ordinary as sneaking a drink and just being silly with some friends.

Another trip with ILP was to a remote summer camp. We all stayed in cabins, doing different crafts and games to spend our days. At the end of that trip, each teen when home with a basket filled with different house supplies. I ended up with a light green laundry basket full of duck bathroom decor. It was cute, not what I would have chosen for myself, but it was one less thing I needed to worry about when I finally moved into my own apartment. Even if I acted as those classes were a pain, I did enjoy most of them and learned a lot. I wish they had more programs to help teens transition out of foster care. The fear of being dumped by the system at eighteen with no support or a family to fall back on if we fail, is a weight all of us wards of the court felt. Some showed fear by doing drugs and failing in school, the pressure too much. On the other hand, I hardened my emotions and stayed laser-focused on being more than a statistic. This was often a determinant to my emotional growth, but at the time, that was okay because feelings made me weak, and I could not allow myself to be vulnerable.

Chapter 27

I turned 17 on May 15th, 2001. It is hard to believe that in just 365 days, I will no longer be a ward of the court and will be able to make my own decisions about my life. This is what I have been waiting for the last four years. I am ready not to be bound to the rules of the state, but I am also terrified that when I fail, I will have no one to help me. I have to figure out how to support myself and continue my education. I do not want to fail and end up jobless or homeless, finding relief in some drugs or alcohol. There are not any programs to help teens transition into adult life. They have programs for those who get in legal trouble or are on drugs. However, those of us who make the right choices are not offered any long-term services to keep us stable. The most I will be able to get help with is my college is paid for by financial aid up to a certain amount because I am a ward of the court, and there is a program to help purchase interview/work clothes. I will take all the help I am offered, hoping it is enough for me to make it. Without Granny, I have no family that would be willing to take me in if I fail. I know Mrs. Tami would help, but she has a life and kids of her own. I would never ask for something so monumental from her. I am grateful she has stuck by my side all these years, even when the system or my attitude made it difficult.

This May, I also finished my first semester of college. I maintained a 3.0-grade point average. I have signed up for two summer classes, Psychology and Spanish I. The Hurds have given me a genuine place to call home. They even worked it out so that I could get my driver's license. At the end of June, I officially was a legal driver, something I thought I could only do once I was eighteen. I am curious to know how they got social services to allow it. I am sure they had to sign papers to take responsibility for me and get car insurance. Even taking the chance to do that for me makes me feel like a true child of theirs. They found a way to make me just like their biological kids. For that, I am grateful. Being treated as a part of a family is a big deal to any foster kid. Who knows at any moment, their world can change. I do not think I will ever understand half of the reasons for my moves over the last three years in care, but it does not matter at this point. In less than a year, I will be free of the system. I fear that my lack of emotional ties will limit my future. Time will tell.

The summer is filled with big changes and lots of new experiences. July comes along, and both Holly and Mike are 18 now, back living with their parents. I have not had as much contact with them in the last few months as I would have liked to. I am worried about them. Some of their choices are not lining up with the future I want. Holly thinks she is pregnant, and Mike was kicked out of his foster home for bad behavior and did not finish high school. I know Holly wants kids, but she is not ready, and I hope she is not pregnant right now. Living with her grandma and having no job is not a good time to have a baby. I told her as much, and she got angry with me. She told me that I think I am better than her because I am in college and finished high school early. I told her that is bull, and she knows it. She is just upset that her life is not going the way she planned. I told her I am not better than anyone; I am just working hard and making different choices, like not having a baby as a teenager. We have had fights before, and I know we will work through it all.

My foster parents allow me to spend the weekend in Sacramento with Holly. It is late July and hot. While I had a blast reconnecting with Holly and Mike, upon returning home, I realized that my loving them both will not be enough to make the friendship with Holly, or my relationship with Mike work. Mike had just been released from jail; he was arrested for drug possession. Holly was getting by living off her grandma. After seeing them as adults and still living the life we always said we did not want, I realized that if I stayed, I would either fall into the same patterns and never make my dreams come true, or I would be working extra hard to be successful and having the weight of taking on other responsibilities. I make the hard choice to break contact with them and end my 2 ½ year relationship with Mike. He is my first love, and the break is a hard one to make. I am hopeful that maybe one day they both with have the life they want, and we could a least be friends again. I feel horrible leaving Holly at such an emotional time in her life, but I cannot let our history keep me bound to our friendship. I want more from life, and I have to cut ties with anyone who doesn't fit that. I hope that I am always able to know when it is the time to move on from people or things that do not have my best interest at heart.

The Hurds spend a lot of time in the summer taking family trips. Something I have never experienced before. That summer, I went camping, four-wheeling, and boating, all for the first time ever. The prep and clean-up for these trips were a lot of work, but I had so much fun. I never thought families could get along and have so much fun outdoors with nothing to distract them from each other. It is not to say everything was perfect because it was not. There were many arguments and attitude issues, especially from us teen girls. I had long-standing issues with one foster sister the most, Vanessa. She had it out for me, and I did not really stick up for myself. She even stole my bank card and stole 600 dollars from me. Dawn told me to stick up for myself, but I did not really see the point since all her trash-talking made others in the house act differently toward me. I just kept my attitude like it did not bother me as much as I could. Even though I was contented living with the Hurds, I kept counting down the days to my 18th birthday. Living in a family that has fights and drama but still accepted and loved one another was too much for me. I wanted that to extend to me, and I am sure it did, but with my past, it was hard to believe.

Time when on, and I continued college and attending IPL classes, where I met Joe. We started officially dating in November. I started working part-time as a cashier at our local department store Mervyn's. I was saving money and still going to Yuba College to work on my Associate's degree. In May of 2002, I turned 18, I celebrated with Joe, and we both got our tongues pierced. We then went back to my foster home for a little get-together. Mrs. Tami came to see me for my 18th birthday with her husband and kids.

They brought me a large teddy bear and a microwave. The summer I turned 18 was the summer I got my first apartment. It was a one-bedroom on the second floor, and Joe and I moved in together. While living with Joe, he lost his job and then got another at McDonalds. In a few weeks time he lost that job as well. I had to put school on hold and work my job at Mervyn's and a night job as a caregiver for Comfort Keepers. We lived together until April 2003. After almost a year of being overworked and not helped by him. I had enough. While he was gone doing who knows what, one day, I had the Hurds help me pack up my apartment. While we were taking things down the stairs, Joe came home and cried and begged me not to leave, that he would have nowhere to go. It was already done, and I told him he is an adult and needs to be one. I was done carrying out our whole relationship. Hell, he was not working and could not even take the trash out, even if I left it in front of our door. He just moved it out of his way to leave the apartment. I was not going to take him back unless he made some major changes. The Hurds, true to their words long ago, let me move back in with them, even though I was 18 and they had no legal responsibility to me.

I was able to quit my second job after moving back in with the Hurds. When I was 19, I started dating a man the Hurds did not approve of. This made a huge issue in the home and with our relationship. Dawn being a former law officer, knew of him and his family's history and warned me he was not a good guy. I did not listen. I ended up moving out of the Hurd's house into an apartment with Dustin. The relationship with Dustin was one-sided. He was using me, and I was too lovesick to do anything about it. I even closed off my relationship with Mrs. Tami for over a year. We had a phone call where she laid it out that I was dating a drug dealer and made a comment regarding my past, and I just cut off contact. The following couple of years, I fought for a relationship with a man in prison. In time after losing a job and starting over alone, I cut off the relationship and focused on myself. The next couple of years is spent working as a Medicare Representative and Appeals Adjuster while finishing my Associate's degree.

Chapter 28

I completed my degree in late 2005, but the
ceremony was held in May 2006. My graduation was
bittersweet. I had made up with Tami at this point because,
let's face it, she was right about my lousy boyfriend. Every
graduate was given two tickets to the ceremony, but I only
needed one. Tami was the only person I wanted to invite,
and she was the only person to show up for me. While I had
my best friend and her family there for support, it was not
just for me, as her sister-in-law was in the same ceremony.

The harsh reality was that I legitimately only had
one person in my life who stayed, no matter my past or
attitude. This realization made me want to investigate the
paternal side of my family. I searched and found my father's

address online. I created a scrapbook of my life and sent it to him. My father, George, called after he received the scrapbook. We had a long conversation, and while I was angry that he never responded to any of the correspondence from social services, I still wanted to know that side of my family. I asked him why he never addressed the letters. He said he never even opened them because he thought my mom was trying to get more child support from him. I never even knew he paid child support. I was pissed because I might not have had to be in foster care if he had answered one letter. It was just another blow of feeling unwanted and like I was too much effort to love. Knowing all of this, I still went out to visit for Christmas and New Year. I wanted to know the aunts, uncles, and cousins I never knew existed. After a phenomenal trip that included three job interviews. I made the huge decision to move to New Jersey.

I returned to California after my trip to finish my notice at my job and clear out my apartment. During that first week in January of 2007, I sold my furniture and packed my green Honda Civic with all of my important things, the rest I trashed. With my over-full car, I started my three-day drive across the country. I took off mid-morning, planning to drive through, stop for gas, and sleep for a few hours each night. I needed to be back in New Jersey and settled to start my new job on the 15th. The drive went well. The late-night driving was challenging. I spent much time on my phone talking to friends to stay awake and avoid my fears. I have never made such a long trip alone, and my sense of direction is horrendous. Equipped with printed map quest directions and snacks, I set off to my new home. The first day and night of the drive were fine; I followed a mac truck to stay in its tracks with the snow falling.

Along the drive Ohio and I had some issues and are not friends. On the third day of driving early morning before dawn, I had to slam on my breaks to avoid hitting another car doing the same. I hit a patch of black ice and was not able to correct it. I fishtailed and ended up tail end into a snow-filled ditch. I was lost at what to do. Luckily a man on his way to work stopped, allowed me to warm up in his car and called a tow truck. Luckily the tow truck came quickly and pulled my car out. I was lucky the car had no damage, and I could continue on my way.

I drove another couple of hours and wanted to stop for gas and a food break. I parked at a truck stop in Ohio. I went inside to use the restroom, and when I stood up to pull up my jeans, my keys which I had in the pocket of my hoodie, fell right into the toilet. That would have been fine, just a gross mess, but no, my luck ran out. It was an automatic flush toilet, and my keys were gone forever. I was shocked and screwed. I had no clue what to do. I wanted to cry like a baby. I did whimper out of frustration. The customer service person helped by trying to get my car unlocked so I could get the VIN to have a key made. I had another man who bought me lunch from Burger King. A few men stopped by to help, but no one could unlock the car. Finally, the truck stop worker called a locksmith. He was able to get me in my vehicle. The worker at the truck stop got approval to drive me a few miles down the road to the local Honda dealer to get a key made. It is a unique electronic key, and I had to pump the break in a pattern to set the key to work for my car. Well, that shit did not work, so in the end, I had to have my vehicle towed to the same dealership that made the key so that they could set the electronic mechanism in the key.

After spending a lot of money between two tows and a locksmith, I was finally on the way out of my new favorite state Ohio. By nightfall, on the third day of my trip, I ended up in Camden, Pennsylvania. I was getting lost, traveling in circles, trying to find the Palmyra Tacony Bridge. I call my dad, who is trying to help, but I feel hopelessly lost. I am hungry and tired, so my crankiness level is on high. I tell him I will park and get some sleep. Instead, he yells at me that young women cannot nap in Camden. It is not safe. I was so aggravated that I did not care. I had been through worse. Finally I find the bridge cross-over, and within minutes I pull into my dad's parking lot. A hot shower and a place to sleep were first on my list.

The next few weeks are spent living on my dad's couch while working and learning about the area. The time staying with him allowed me to get to know him and his wife, Penny. Things were not easy, and my past reared its ugly head. My shameful disguised secret would become painfully outed. I thought finding my family would mean finding myself and leaving my demons behind. I am sad to say it does not work that way. One evening after dinner at my dad's house, I went to the bathroom to purge, but it went too far this time. I was using a toothbrush to help myself throw up and went too far down my throat with it. I lost grip on the end of the toothbrush and accidentally swallowed it. I knew I had to get medical attention, so I had to share my secret. I told Penny what had happened, and she asked if I do this often.

I said only when I am in an emotional overload. Penny went on and on about how it is wrong to do that to my body. I had told Penny and my Dad when I moved in with them that I did have issues related to my past. However, I never sat down and told them what the problems were. The bingeing and purging started about a year before my move to New Jersey. I had another failed relationship. My best friend and I were fighting. I was not talking to Tami much.

I felt lost, alone, and worthless. I let all the degrading things my mother told me as a young girl and teen play on repeat in my head. All of those horrible feelings had nowhere to go. Bingeing and purging occasionally allowed me to feel in control of my life and rid the destructive emotions. My habit was not a daily thing. I could go weeks without an episode until my emotions overwhelmed me, and I needed the outlet. I believe my physical appearance never changed since I was not doing it after all my meals to lose weight. There were no outward signs of an issue until the evening I swallowed the toothbrush.

Penny took me to the local emergency room, where I wrote on the check-in why I was there. The clerk made a point to come out to me in the waiting room to make sure what I wrote was correct and to ask if I was in pain, which I was not. I was eventually triaged and then transferred to another hospital that could manage my case. I spent the night and was taken back to the operating room for a scope procedure to retrieve the toothbrush in the morning. When I was in recovery, they stated they were almost not able to remove the toothbrush by the scope and would have had to open me up. I believe the doctors suspected an eating disorder, but with my story and no other physical symptoms, they could do nothing about it. I was released later that afternoon with a sore throat and a ruff voice. Those symptoms would last a few days. I took the light rail from Philly into New Jersey, where Penny picked me up and took me home. The next few days, my dad and stepmom were tense and awkward. They could not understand my actions, and I did not want to discuss the issue anymore. My past, which my dad could have saved me from had he wanted to be a parent, had lasting effects on me.

I eventually found a place to rent with three other women. We all rented the upstairs of a converted convent in

Collingswood. Collingswood is a small historic town just a light rail away from Philadelphia. Getting to know the girls' bar hopping and working are some of my best memories. I started working at a title company where my roommate Vic worked. Vic helped me find my love for being active and going to the gym. Occasionally, I still purged, but I kept that secret from my roommates.

We were more about fun, and I wanted to maintain the vibe of the house. Time passed, and I dated a bit, keeping things casual and fun. I wanted to find myself and settle into my new life without the complication of a committed relationship. I was twenty-two, and fun was what I craved. Unfortunately, things do not always work out the way we plan. My carefree and fun lifestyle was on the way out the door.

October 2007 rolled around, and I found myself staring at a positive pregnancy test at the age of twenty-three.

My roommate Vic was waiting in my bright yellow bedroom across the hall from the bathroom and hounding me for the results. The test was positive before I had the cap back on and sat it down to set the timer. I knew right then that no matter what anyone else had to say on the subject, I would have my baby. I have always dreamed of being a mom and being better than the one I had. This was my chance. My roommate Vic and I talked about all of my options, but she knew I would be having the baby. She told me of her abortion experience, and while I am not against abortion, it was just not the right choice for me. I had my first OBGYN visit in early November and confirmed my pregnancy. I then had to work up the courage to tell my family. My roommates accepted the baby, but there was space logistics since I had the smallest room in the house, being the last roommate to move in. I was too cowardly to call my dad to tell him, so I texted him, and he replied, "and I just saved a ton of money switching to Geico." I text him back that I was not joking and that I was due June 21, 2008. He replied, "Well, as long as the baby is not Black, if it is mixed, it is not my grandchild. That comment was the start of the end of our relationship. My aunts both tried to get me to have an abortion or to go the adoption route. I called Tami one evening to tell her the news. She was out at Taco Bell with one of her sons when she took my call. I was worried about what she would say and think, especially with my family's reactions. I told her, and her response was congratulations. I started to cry because she was the only person to tell me that. I am happy about having the baby. I wanted those around me to be happy too.

My pregnancy progresses, and I find out I am having a girl, whom I named Alexia Grace after my sister. My pregnancy is smooth even though I am considered high risk for preterm labor and fetal growth restriction. I continue to work up until four weeks before my due date. The last week

I am working, I find out I will not have a job to return to after my maternity leave. Since I had not worked at the job a full year before I needed to take leave, they did not have to hold my position for me, and FMLA did not apply. I was terrified at the thought of being single and jobless with a new baby, but I would find a way. I was thrown a small baby shower at my job before I went on leave and then another by my family in the summer. The baby shower was thrown by my stepmom Penny. While I had a great time, and my baby was blessed with needed items. Family drama occurred. Penny was upset that I allowed and wanted my cousin's children at the shower, and she swears at the end of the party that I did not thank her for hosting. I did with a hug and all, which my Aunt Linda witnessed. It did not matter to Penny; she cut off contact with me.

My water broke on June 19, and I labored for a few hours, given Pitocin, and made no progress. Finally, Alexia's heart rate when too high, and an emergency c-section was required. Alexia Grace was born on June 20, 2008. Holding her for the first time, I knew what true love was. My roommate Vic was with me the whole time, and she was the second person to hold her. My aunt Linda and Uncle Grady drove up to visit us in the hospital. They loved her at first sight too. I texted my dad, but he and my stepmom were too concerned about going to Sonic on their way home from a camping trip to stop and meet their granddaughter. I do not know if that was more Penny's choice or if my dad did not care either way. We are released four days later; Vic brings us home. There I find a new way of living by the demands of a newborn. Vic was an immense help in the early days, as I was not able to move around well, healing from my c-section. Alexia was a couple of weeks old when my dad finally came to my place to meet her. I all but had to toss her at him to get him to hold her. About three minutes later, I had her back in my arms and had lost my dad's interest altogether. Before I knew it, my dad was off to my roommate's bedroom, getting high. I was pissed. Was getting high more paramount to my dad than my child? The pattern fits. He was never there for me. Why did I want more when it came to my baby?

The next few weeks go by in a blur of diapers and feedings. Things are not well with me. I am having awful thoughts about Lexi. I had thought of throwing her out of my third-story window. I wanted to hurt her at all times. I had many other ideas of hurting her. I never did. I wounded myself instead. I was able to release the built-up emotions for a short time after I cut myself. I thought of purging even though I had not had an episode since I discovered I was pregnant. I told my doctor my thoughts and actions at my six-week checkup, requesting help. I asked for help, knowing I did not want to hurt my baby.

The doctor steps out of the room for a long while, I knew something was up, and I was correct. Even though I did nothing wrong and asked for help, they called the authorities on me. I was given a choice to commit myself voluntarily or be committed. I wanted help but did not want to be away from my baby. I was a mess torn on the inside. I did not want my baby in the system. They advised me I could contact my family to take her. I was taken by ambulance to the hospital, where therapists talked to me. They tried calling my aunts and could not contact them right away. That, in turn, had them calling social services to get involved. The thing I feared more than anything. I was finally able to get a hold of my Aunts, and they both drove up with my uncle to get Alexia and my keys to get her things from my apartment. Even though my family took her, and I knew she would be loved and cared for, I was devastated. I did not know when I would see my baby again.

Once my baby was gone with my family, I was searched and admitted to the local hospital until they found a bed in a facility to hold me until my commitment was completed. I was taken to a room with a low bed with no blankets or sheets, and a metal chair bolted to the floor in the corner under the phone. I had no belongings and was locked in the room, with only a small square window in the door to look through. The rest of the room was painted a pale cream white, with nothing to do and no contact with anyone. I felt like a prisoner doing time in the hole for unruly behavior. I cried for hours curled up on the chair because the bed with no bedding felt too exposed. A few hours later, an ambulance was ready to transport me to the facility where I would be treated. It is after midnight when I get a check-in. I am too exhausted to take much in and fall into bed and drift off quickly. A nurse wakes me to get ready for medication and breakfast. I am given my first dose of an antidepressant ever. I am not hungry, but some other patients tell me to eat, or it looks bad and goes against a person in treatment. The next couple of days are spent with many hours of individual and group therapy sessions. I cry a lot, missing my baby. I have no idea how long they will keep me away from her. My aunt and cousin bring me some clothes and toiletries. While they are at the hospital, I get a quick glimpse of Lexi via the window in the double doors. I want to hold her so badly. I am very grateful my Aunt Linda took Lexi in. I would have hated for her to have to go into foster care. However, I am terrified that asking for help will be detrimental to me being able to parent Lexi.

There is talk of me having a long-term commitment in Anocora. I do not feel being sent to a hard-core mental hospital is what I need. If I have to go there, I think it would be what finally breaks me. Also, that type of place is not always safe. The patients can be violent at times. I am lucky to be released after a few days as long as I live with my aunt. She agrees to supervise my parenting Lexi and allow me to live with her. The doctor had to report me to child services for the thought of harming my baby. Even though I was, I was there asking for help. The next few weeks are spent getting used to my antidepressant and dealing with the requirements of the department of child services. Gwen is our case worker, and while I like her, I am not a fan of her supervisor. She seems out to get me and to find a way to permanently take my baby away from me. I start weekly therapy sessions and maintain my meds. I loathe therapy, but I have no choice but to do it or face losing my baby. I am diagnosed with postpartum depression and PSTD. I am genuinely enjoying the summer at my aunt's home, and it is very nice to have help with the baby.

A couple of months in, I realize I hate Prozac; I have no emotions or feelings at all. My doctor changes my medication, and I feel better emotionally. Thankfully, it does not make me hungry all the time. I have a home visit done at my apartment, which is cleared and deemed safe for the baby. It took just over four months to fully live on my own with Lexi and for child services to close the case. About halfway through the time I was staying with my aunt, the Child services supervisor sent a letter to my apartment, which she knew I was not staying at, saying they substantiated the claim of abuse and or neglect. It would be on my record forever. If I wanted to appeal, I could. Unfortunately, since she purposely sent the letter to the incorrect address, I missed the deadline to submit an appeal. I learned of the letter from my case worker Gwen, who informed me that her supervisor wanted to permanently remove the baby. She cited my childhood as a reason, even though I asked for help and did everything they requested. This supervisor had judged me on the sins of another, just like most of the people in the system when I was a kid. I will never understand why so many people in my past and this case do not believe I can be better and break the cycle of abuse. I might understand it some if I had in the past used drugs or got in some trouble. But here I am, doing my best and being a stable adult but getting punished anyway. I looked for a way to have the case overturned, but I was met with a brick wall and threats along the way. In the end, I just decided to be glad that the case was closed and I was able to raise Lexi.

Since I was unemployed and could live on my savings and unemployment pay, I decided to return to school. I chose an online program with Herzing University. I started classes to obtain another A.A. degree, this time with a focus on Medical Billing. I spent the next few months going to school and taking time to be with family. They all adored baby Lexi.

Chapter 29

In early 2009 my Aunt Linda convinced me to submit an inquiry to the Dr. Phil show. By March 2009, a production crew was tapping my story and other scenes at my aunt's home in Ship Bottom, New Jersey. They followed me to the end of the street over, looking at the bay, getting those dramatic shots for the show. It was odd to be filmed trying to act normal and do everyday things like take Lexi to the park. None of the production effects were natural or normal. I never knew so much work and tapping was done before actually being on the show. About a week later, Linda, Lexi, and I were on a flight from Philly to LAX. I was concerned a baby on a six-hour flight would be horrible, but she was good, and the other people on the plane also loved her. When we landed, we were chauffeured to a hotel on the strip. We could see the Hollywood sign outside the window of our room. It is funny all the years I lived in California; I had never been to Hollywood.

That first day we met up with Tami, saw some local sites, and had dinner. Lexi was nine months old and learned how to pull herself up to stand in the back in play in the hotel room. She smiled so big and was so proud of herself. The next day was full of hair and makeup, and I felt like a hooker being so made up. T.V. makeup is no joke. I did not even meet Dr. Phil until the actual show. The segment was tapped quickly. The introduction was the scenes filmed prior to the show. I gave brief history run down and talked about foster care and having a CASA worker. Tami spoke a few words as well. The episode was called Caught in the System. At the end of the show, a sponsor the show found paid for my associate's degree with Herzing University, and JC Penny sponsored a crib and bedding for Lexi. I did not expect compensation for being on the show. I just wanted a chance to get my story out to the public.

After the taping, we took pictures with Dr. Phil and his wife. After being transported back to the hotel, we did some more sightseeing. We saw the stars on the Hollywood walk of fame, hit some local shops, and went to Ripley's Believe it or not. It was great to spend time with Tami. After a nice dinner out, we called it a night. The next day was the flight home back to reality.

Chapter 30

Regular ordinary life resumed taking online classes, working as a medical biller while completing my internship, my relationship with Rob progressing, and being a parent to an active toddler. Rob and I moved in with his parents briefly while looking for our own home to rent. His parents are great, and love having Lexi around. Things are getting tough having a toddler in the house with Anne, Rob's mom, and her progressing Alzheimer's. We did not want to move so soon, but having a small child in the home seemed to agitate Anne's conditions. We decided to stay until the new year. That way, we could have a family Christmas while Anne could hopefully be present and enjoy it. With things being settled and stable, Rob and I decided to start trying for baby number two. During this wonderfully mundane time in my life, Barbara went up for her first attempt at parole. I was not made aware of the hearing until after the fact. I was informed by a news article Tami showed me after the parole hearing stating that on her hearing dated 2-27-2009, Barbara was denied for five years. I was pleased with her being denied and was angry I was not notified of the hearing or the outcome. I was never told as a teen that, as a victim, I would have to request to be notified of any hearings or death of Barbara and Larry. I immediately contacted California's parole board online and requested notification regarding my victim rights.

In August 2010, I completed my 2nd associate's degree with a focus on Medical Billing and Coding. Months and then years go by with nothing traumatic or eventful happening. Rob is working as a Chef on Long Beach Island, Lexi is in pre-school, and I am still working part-time while trying to complete my Bachelor's degree. We are having no luck getting pregnant with baby number two. I am unbelievably depressed over it, but we are not in any position to seek medical help to have a baby. So while things are good and we are happy, we are like most couples living paycheck to paycheck.

Chapter 31

One afternoon in early March of 2012, Rob and I were home. I worked part-time, and Rob did not have a contracting job that day. There was a knock at the door. This was not normal for us, as we did not have people just dropping by. I was very against drop-by visits by anyone. My home is my safe place, and having it invaded without my prior approval was too much for my emotional state. I went down the stairs of our split-level rental and opened the front door to a woman with wildly curly brown hair and a sweet smile. She had a file folder in her hand, and even with the friendly facade, I was set on edge. She explained to us that an anonymous call was placed to child services.

The unidentified person stated they saw me with a hypodermic needle in my mouth at the bus stop with my almost-four-year-old. I laughed at the women because even a full-on drug addict would not do something so dumb knowing they could be seen by official employees of their child's school. I told them I have never done any drugs but some pot as a teenager. Then the bullshit occurred. Because of the substantiated abuse case when Lexi was six weeks old (my postpartum request for help), she had to do more than interview the family. I was once again being punished for my mothers' choices. I was then put through the wringer with a scheduled and random drug test. I offered to pay for the one where they test hair since that test can show years of drug use, but I was denied.

One afternoon I drove an hour to Toms River to the child services office for a drug test. That one was fine; besides getting lost because I am terrible with directions, I did not feel judged or disrespected during the drug test. A few days later, the social worker stops by again with another woman for the random drug test. While I was thrilled to have this done and closer to closing the case, the drug test administrator was a crotchety ass of a woman. I was trying to stay calm and get the test done so they could leave my home. The social was sweet and told me this is what I was waiting for so the case can be closed. I agreed with her but did not appreciate how the other woman treated me. I go into my bathroom with three people, the test administrator, the social worker, and Rob, watching me pee. I give my sample and set it on my countertop. I wash my hands and go to leave when the testing woman yells at me to stop and put the lid on the sample. Then give it to her. I lost it on her and yelled back that I did not care that she hates her job and life, but a little prior instruction would be nice, since I had never done this before. She huffed at me and mumbled something under her breath. I told her to take the sample and get out of my house. She should still be professional and not judgmental because she deemed me guilty. The sweet social worker got her to leave. She stayed behind for a few and apologized for the women's behavior. She also informed me that her investigation found no abuse or neglect, and as long as the drug test is negative, the case would be closed unfounded. A couple of weeks later, I received a letter in the mail stating the case was closed. I was relieved because I once again proved myself worthy of being Lexi's mother.

I found out who made the call. I will forever bear the scars left behind from the fear of my child being taken from me. The caller turned out to be a woman who lives a street over. She had a choice as to which street she wanted to use for the bus stop, as they did not stop on her street. Mind you. I would walk to the bus stop with my German Shepard on her leash. She said she did not like my dog and that dogs scared her child. I told her I would not stop bringing my dog as she had done nothing wrong. I offered that we stay on opposite sides of the street while waiting for the bus, but she disagreed, and I just told her that it is not even her bus stop. She can go to the other bus stop. According to the social worker, this same woman makes many calls to child services when she has issues with people. When I turned 18 and became a legal adult, I thought my interaction with child services would be done. I knew the right things to do and had a good life I was building. I never wanted my baby exposed to the system. I am grateful that in both of these events with child services, with a bit of work on my part, I proved myself, the cases were dropped, and my child was never taken from my care. However, I feel persecuted and judged in both instances by so-called professionals without all the facts. I will always have some part of me that fears any child I have could be taken from me forever. The system worked correctly in my two cases, but I have seen in my childhood when they make the wrong decisions.

Chapter 32

In my couple year-long hunt for full-time work, I finally found a full-time billing position for a Podiatrist. Although, I quit my part-time job of over three years, my boss was upset and wanted me to stay on part-time with different hours so I could still take this new job. I was a bit offended that I was a good enough employee to keep on part-time but not give more hours. Ultimately, I quit because having two jobs would not work well with kids and my online classes. At this point, it had been about two years of trying for a baby. Rob and I decided to give up the dream of another baby and focus on our careers so we could buy a home soon. Plus, having dealt with child services again, I was leery of the idea of bringing in another baby that could be taken from me. With that, I started working and learned so much so fast. The physician I was working for taught me how to use the program and all of the ins and outs of podiatry billing. I took to the job quickly, cleaned up her account, and was praised for bringing in old money. I was positively proud of my success in my new position.

After about two months of working for Dr. Irina, I discovered I was pregnant. I was in total shock. I had a feeling I was pregnant but wanted to wait a couple of weeks to test. I did not want to test too early and be let down. I got up early on June 2, 2012, and took a test. Ecstatic with the positive result, I went into the living room, gave Rob the test, and said Happy Birthday. It was very early, so we were both in a daze with the information. I stayed with him for a few on the couch but decided sleep was better. I went back to bed, and he went to work.

My pregnancy was progressing Rob, and I are working a lot. I obtained my bachelor's degree in August 2012. I was worried I would be terminated from my job because, with my first pregnancy, I was since I did not work with the company a year before I needed leave. However, my second pregnancy is turning out the same way; Dr. Irina said I would not be fired. November rolls around, and Lexi is sick. She ends up needing a couple of days in the hospital. While we are admitted, the doctors determined Lexi has an umbilical hernia that needs repair. We schedule her surgery for the week before my scheduled c-section. I planned to have Lexi all healed and settled before I needed my own recovery time. Well, our second baby disagreed with the plan. Lexi's surgery was scheduled for January 17, 2013, and my c-section was scheduled for the 23rd. I woke up with contractions on the morning of the 16th, and my water had broken. Rob took me to the hospital, and I arranged with a friend to get Lexi from daycare. As I wait to return to the operating room, I get the phone call to confirm Lexi's surgery is at seven in the morning. The woman and I both had a laugh about my new little one's timing. My c-section is complication-free, and Rob and I have a beautiful little girl Marie-Elena Cooper Reis. Life with a 4-year-old and newborn is difficult, but I feel blessed.

Chapter 33

On June 13, 2014, Barbara has another parole hearing. This time I was notified, and I attend via my cell phone. I had many feelings leading up to the hearing. I almost backed out more than once. I was most afraid of hearing Barbara's voice. I wanted to be able to speak my mind and do everything I could to keep her in prison for what she did to Alexia and I. I wanted to show her I am successful and happy to spite her. I also wanted to make up for being too scared to speak at her sentencing. I did not know what to expect regarding how the hearing would go or how long it would last. The board went over her crimes and her behavior while in prison. Overall, I learn she is a model prisoner with only one infraction for having another inmate's property.

The board spends a lot of time going over her accomplishments. Barbara Completed her high school diploma in 2006 and a two-year degree in 2013. She had worked in the prison's optical unit for 12 years with great remarks from her supervisor. If released, Barbara obtained her optical technician certificate and plans to work in that field.

Throughout her prison stay starting in 2000, Barbara has taken many self-help classes ranging from an Attitude and Self-esteem course to Narcotics Anonymous. The board asked Barbara about her plans after release. She was accepted to three different halfway homes. Barbara told the committee that she would continue NA and avoid being around other users. Her outside support persons were listed as well. Barbara also noted her newfound relationship with God being a devout Christian now, would aid in her success on the outside. When the board asked her about the crimes she committed, why she failed to demonstrate acceptance of her part in the crime, and genuine remorse for her actions. Barbara, at the hearing, blamed the murder of Alexia on Chad. According to Barbara, after speaking with Chad (who was six at the time), he told her to use bleach to rid the demons. Barbara also stated that Larry was the mastermind behind most of the ill-treatment.

After the board thoroughly reviewed her history and her plans for future success, the lawyers for both sides gave a closing argument as to why she should be approved or denied parole. Barbara's lawyer noted her trouble-free time in prison as well as her educational successes. The prosecution leads more with the horrible nature of the crime and Barbara's lack of remorse. I was allowed to speak. I was so nervous I talked too fast. I addressed many of the lies Barbara had told in her testimony. I spoke of my successes and how I accomplished them all in spite of her. I told of how my parenting of my two daughters is affected by her lack of compassion and love for her children. In the end, I stated that my sister would never get to have any of the accomplishments I have, I will never have a relationship with my sister, my children will never have an aunt, and I will never get to be an aunt to Alexia's children. We will never know who Alexia could have been, and until Barbara can bring her back to life and give her all Alexia had lost, she does not deserve to be released from prison.

After all of the closing speeches, the board took a short recess to determine whether Barbara would be approved for parole. The wait for the board to call me back to hear the results was about 40 minutes, but it felt like hours. I was sick to my stomach and wanted to know if her release would forever torment my life. Once all participants were back in the room or on the phone, the board listed the reasons for their decision. Barbara's lack of taking certain self-help classes and failure to plan for possible triggers on the outside was listed. They also listed her lack of taking full responsibility for her actions and lack of remorse as their reasons for denying her request for parole at that time. The parole board could only deny her for three years as she was a model prisoner without infractions to warrant a longer term. My relief was instant, and I felt very vindicated. Of course, I would like her to be denied for a longer time, but at least I had won this battle of the war. I am determined to live my life to the fullest and be happy, not thinking about the next time I will have to face this same battle.

Chapter 34

In late 2015, I am thirty-one. Life is good, but I am down. I know I should be happy things are stable. I am working full-time for Traknet Medical Billing. I have been working there for almost two years at this point. Rob is still working as a chef during the spring and summer seasons and as a contractor during winter. Our girls are great. Lexi is seven and doing well in elementary school. Marie-Elena is almost three years old and loving daycare and all her little toddler friends. Something is missing. I have not had much contact with my family as of late. I have not spoken to my father since Lexi's first birthday. He was angry with me for not inviting him to her first birthday, but there was so much animosity between his wife and me. I did not want to bring any drama to a one-year-old party. I was not as close with my dad anymore. His actions when Lexi was a newborn and the lack of contact that year changed our relationship. I have found that with my past, I can easily put an end to relationships that are damaging to my kids or me. Rob noticed I was off and depressed and said I know what you need. We should have another baby. I had always wanted to have many kids; Rob was happy with our two. We decided to try for one more baby, hopefully, a boy this time. Since it took almost two years to get pregnant with Marie-Elena, I thought we would be trying for around the same amount of time. Boy, I was so wrong. Two months later, I was staring at a positive pregnancy test. I showed Rob, and he said, hell, take another one that cannot be right. The second test showed the same thing. We were being blessed with another baby.

The pregnancy was progressing well. I was due December 6, 2016. I have always been lucky with no significant pregnancy symptoms. My most aggravating symptom was constantly being tired. Life continued with a nice routine. I was always considered high risk with my pregnancies, so I had extra care. On one such visit, about 16 weeks pregnant, I had a growth check ultrasound where they found a cyst in the fetus's brain. While the doctor stated it can be a normal occurrence that would clear up before birth, it could also indicate a chromosomal issue incompatible with life, such as Trisomy 13. I was terrified, and being alone at this specific visit made me feel worse. The doctor suggested a blood test to confirm either way. The blood was taken, and then the wait for results began. The week of waiting almost gave me an ulcer. I wanted nothing more than to have a healthy baby. I did not want to have to make a choice to terminate if the baby had an issue not compatible with life.

At the gas station, I got a call from my high-risk doctor, stating that the baby is completely healthy and testing shows I am having another little girl. I walked back to my car, got inside to call Rob, and tell him the news. After speaking with Rob, I hung up, closed my eyes, and cried. I allowed all the stress and tension to release with my tears.

After learning she would be fine, we decided on a name for our newest family member. Samantha Antoinette will be joining us in a few short months. I reach viability in my pregnancy at the wondrous 24-week mark. I was off one day, and I started having contractions. I had never experienced true contractions before. I was worried it was too soon. I went to my doctor for a check-up, and I was determined to be having preterm labor and needed to not work or work from home on modified bed rest. I was allowed to work from home with the help of my immediate manager. Speaking up for my work ethic and how much I handle in accounts, corporate approved the request. Allowing me to work from home was beneficial to both parties. I would not have to take disability and lose some income, and Traknet would not have to find someone to cover my accounts. With modified bed rest, I was able to continue my pregnancy until just after the 36-week mark. I started with contractions again, even though I was just under four weeks early. My doctor decided not to stop my labor. I was taken back for a c-section and, as I requested to have my Fallopian tubes removed. Rob and I had decided that with all of the complications and my kidney disease that this would be our last baby. The risk to my health and the risk of preterm labor was too much to even think of having a fourth baby.

On the afternoon of November 9, 2016, Sammy was born. She had trouble breathing from being just a bit too early and needed a NICU stay. I left the hospital four days after the birth without my baby. I was hysterical, leaving my newborn behind. While rationally, I knew she needed medical care. My heart did not understand why she was not with me. I drove the 45-minute drive every day for the next four days to spend the day with Samantha in the NICU. Finally, on the eighth day, she was released, and my newborn finally met her big sisters. The big girls were so excited that Sam was finally home. Life was already full, but adding a newborn to the mix took some time for us all to adjust. With her birth, I finally felt that our family was complete.

Chapter 35

Around Christmas time, Tami flew in from California to meet the new baby. She stayed at a local hotel as our rental home was too small, and we had no room for her to stay. The couple-day visit went by too fast. Lexi cried for a long while on her last day, not wanting her to go. Besides Rob's dad, she was the only family to visit to see our new addition. I am enjoying my maternity leave while also trying to heal from delivery. I take Sammy to my work to meet the Traknet crew. She is passed around in a whirl of baby snuggles. I am not looking forward to returning to work in the office and putting the baby in daycare, but that is the life of this working mom.

My eight-week leave does not seem long enough. I am in the process of getting life rearranged so that I can go back to work when I meet challenges from the human resources department. They failed to complete my disability paperwork correctly, causing a delay in my funds. I email and call with no results to get the paperwork redone. I am getting a lot of pushback, telling me it is my fault since I should have taken disability leave when I had preterm labor. This ensues an argument because I was given approval to work from home instead of taking leave. I am hormonal and tired, giving me a short fuse. I am not friendly to the women in human resources. A couple of frustrated emails later, my paperwork is finally completed correctly. But at this rate, I will not receive my payment until after I return to work. This is a mess, and I have bills to pay. There is no one in the local office that can help. I am lost. About a week later, I receive a phone call from the corporate office informing me that my employment was being terminated. When I inquire into why they state New Jersey is an at-will employment state and they did not need a reason. I was a good employee who handled more accounts than others. I did not understand.

I was fired while on maternity leave, and around the same time, Rob had issues with his manager at the restaurant, and he determined he was not going back to work in such an environment. So, there we are with three kids and no income. I did not know what to do. We set up a go fund me just to be able to make rent for January. Rob was working his contracting job, but one income was not enough. I went head first into trying to find another job, which is hard to do with a newborn at home. Rob tried to convince me to open my own billing company, but I was scared. I did not want to fail. I am educated and knowledgeable in the medical field. I did not know where to start to create my own company, and my fear was holding me back. In the end, the choice was made for me.

A few weeks into my emotional spiral, I was contacted by Dr. Megara. I had done his billing for almost three years while I worked at Traknet. He called because he was unhappy with whoever was doing his billing within Traknet. He knew I was terminated and asked what I would charge to do his billing from home. We discussed rates, and I created a contract while he gave notice to Traknet to terminate services. While waiting the 30 days for him to finish his contract with Traknet Billing, I obtained all the equipment I would need, set up a 1-800 line for patients to call, and became an officially licensed company in the state of New Jersey. On February 11, 2017, Advanced Specialty Medical Billing was official and in production.

While the income from having one client was excellent, we needed more to support us. I started to reach out with advertising via email from a contact list I had obtained of Traknet using providers. A few weeks in, Kim from Dr. Shorts' office contacted me, asking me also to do their billing. She missed me from Traknet and was not satisfied with her new point of contact, and their income was also down. With some word of mouth and the emails I sent out, I added another client to ASM Billing. I went from being fired with no hope to a business owner making almost three times what I had been at Traknet within a four-month time period. Time went by, and the business was booming. We were able to pay off debt and start saving to purchase a home. I could also keep Sammy at home, with no daycare for her. With some luck and hard work, a situation that could have been devastating to my family turned into one of the best things to happen to our family.

Chapter 36

On May 3, 2017, I attended Barbara's parole hearing by phone. The hearing starts the same as the others. The board reviews her prison history, addresses any new classes she has completed and determines the line of questioning. Barbara, at this time, addresses the board, trying to give them whatever information they are looking for so she can be released. She states she is responsible for her part in Alexia's death, but in the same sentence, it was Larry who gave her the final dose of the bleach milkshake. Barbara states she told Larry to call the cops, but he was against it because he did not want to go to jail. She also says she did CPR with chest compression. Bearing witness to my sister's death, I know her words are untrue. Then the board dives into her plan for release. The different housing communities she was accepted into, her job, and relapse prevention plans. She has started taking Judaism classes and working with a Rabbi to convert her religion. According to her, this religion is peaceful and does not believe in demons.

The board goes over her letters of support and against. There is a letter from my brother Chad against her release. Barbara states she has no contact with him and did not know he was in opposition to her release. She has three support letters, her sponsor, her brother, and her ex-husband Charles. I cannot fathom ever supporting her release, but Alexia's own father is in support of her murder being free. As a parent, I do not think I would ever be able to support the person who took my child's life, maybe if it was some freak accident, but it would be challenging. They also did not have the most stable marriage, so I am not sure how he would be a good support person now. The board questions that as well, but Barbara says that it would only be a friendship now, and that would allow them to have a healthy relationship.

In closing statements this round, Barbara states the following. "Today, I want to acknowledge Alexia's life. I am here to attempt to bring closure to the murder I have committed. I owe this to my family members and everyone who is sitting before me. You are the people I keep in mind when I find the incentive to keep doing what is right by becoming a better woman. What I have accomplished is important in my personal growth, although it can never be more important than Alexia's life and will not bring her back. I cannot change the decision I made that day. I now live my life honoring Alexia's life by mentoring the young lifers, helping the less fortunate, working towards a college degree, staying sober and clean, faithfully attending NA meetings, and taking self-help groups for my own personal growth. I continue working on my emotions, such as anger, shame, guilt, hurt, and rejection, by expressing my feelings to communicate them more effectively. I work on my sobriety through fellowship, journalism, prayer, and daily reflections. Today, I take the time to make better decisions without responding in impulsive matters, and I think about the consequences of my actions rather than resorting to quick solutions. I continue to stay involved in self-help groups because I feel that healing is a continuing process. I live my journey and living amends by devoting time to women who have the same struggles with self-forgiveness. My prayer is that you are able to recognize the changes that I have made and not by my past choices. And I just want to thank everyone at this time."

My closing statement, "Um, I am really thankful for the mute button on my phone because there were so many times I wanted to yell out because her story is just that. It's a story. It's not what happened. She's telling you whatever she thinks she can tell you, so you'll release her with those fake tears. It was never about being sorry about what she did, it is about being sorry that she is not getting to live the life she wanted to, but you know what, neither am I. Neither are my siblings. She is the one. Larry is not the one who placed my sister in the bathtub, put the enema in her, and watched her die. Larry was sitting at the dining room table, forcing me to drink the bleach cocktail while she was in the bathroom doing whatever she was doing to my sister, and then she pulled her out. I could see around the corner and attempted to resuscitate her, but not really. She did that, and you want to keep blaming someone else. There is no reason to be out. You know, stay where you are. Nobody wants you out, and your people who are there to support you, these people you met— (at this point, I am told by the board not to direct my comments to Barbara)- Okay. Well, even still, the people, her former husband, he—how could you forgive her for murdering your child? And he did stuff to me, abusive when they were separating, so what kind of person is he to be a support t person to help someone stay on the straight and narrow? I mean, I understand California laws are changing. I understand that she may not be deemed violent anymore, but it doesn't change the fact that she was, and what happens if she relapses? What happens if she decides she is going to try to find her kids, who do not want anything to do with her, and we do not get notified that she's coming? I personally do not want to deal with a surprise visit. That is something I cannot handle. I don't want her around my children. I don't want the lies. I don't – It affects me. I'm proud, okay? Good for her. She went to high school. She is going to college. She is doing all these things. Yay. She is in an institution where she has no other choice. You do that or go to the SHU or wherever they put you if you don't listen, so yeah—where is my self-help? Where is my college education? Where are all of those things for me? I've done it myself, with no help from her. I raised myself and raised my siblings when they were around. We did it all on our own. I am a mother and a business owner. I have a degree and have done all of that without her help. And she still gets to sit there, lie to all of you, and pretend to cry? Uh, I'm sorry, there are so many notes I have heard that I could go on and on, but there is really no point, just the fact that she did lie about many things. There was no flood in the house, so she had to change the carpets. She altered the carpet because she got body pieces on there. And they needed to bleach the carpets and the floors. Okay? My sister was tied to a chair with duct tape in the closet for days at a time before she died. And she was cut up in that closet. So, they ripped the linoleum out, bleached the floors, and replaced it. All the meanwhile, oh, she doesn't know whether I was there or if I came in and happened to see it. No, I was there. They made me sit there. From the day she died, they told me—the story they made up that she lived in Chicago with her father, and they advised me if I didn't go along with the story, I was going to end up just like her. So no, it wasn't some magical thing that just happened, and she doesn't know why it happened. There was thinking, whether they were high or not, they were still thinking of a process of a way to get away with murdering her. With putting her body in the fire and putting her ashes in the river. You know, there's no body. There is no memorial. There is nobody there. Nobody cares enough to give my sister what she deserves. And she's still lying. So, I mean, there is really nothing else I have to say. I'm sorry.

The board then took a recess to make their decision. About a half hour goes by, and they call me back to resume the hearing. The commission found her unsuitable for release, listing her lack of insight into the crime and what led her to the horrendous crime that took her daughter's life. We found you minimizing today, just telling us what you wanted us to hear as opposed to just laying it all out for the board. They found her relapse prevention plan lacking. In spite of the doctor's risk assessment, the Panel does not find significant evidence of positive rehabilitation with convinces that if released, you will not pose a potential threat to public safety. Thus not suitable for parole, and this is a three-year denial.

Chapter 37

With the stress of the hearing behind me, I focus on growing my business. Over the next year, by word of mouth, I am able to add another client. ASM billing is a success in my book. I am finally where I always wanted to be. I never had dreams of being rich. I wanted to be successful with my family and career. I wanted to make enough money to support my family while being able to do some fun things from time to time. My mother never took me to do simple things like the movies, ice cream dates, amusement parks, or anything of the like. I wanted to be able to do that for my kids. Small things lead to significant memories. One of the first things that made me truly believe I made it was I could close the office one day and surprise my girls with a trip to the zoo. Just a random day of fun. Before, I could never afford to do something like that. By June 2018, we were pre-approved for a mortgage. It was time to go house shopping. Rob and I knew we wanted to move from New Jersey to a state with better taxes for small business owners. We also wish for the best school district we can find for our girls. This leads us to search in the Clarks Summit area of Pennsylvania. Our requirements for our future home were simply an acre or more of land, a bedroom for each of the girls, and a space for Rob's dad to live with us. Grandpa was getting older and living alone, him moving with us would be the best choice to be able to care for him. We found our dream home and were set to close at the end of August.

While our dream of owning a family home was finally happening after years of hard work and struggles, Grandpa would not be moving with us. That summer, his health turned for the worst almost overnight. He was diagnosed with Alzheimer's and then fell ill. We found out at that point it was lung cancer. Knowing Grandpa's condition as it was, he would not have wanted to try to treat the cancer. We spent the summer caring for him in his last weeks. He never made it to see the house we chose in person, but we knew he would have been happy for us. He passed the first week of August. During the month, we spent time cleaning out Grandpa's home. On August 26, we closed on our home, but the next week we moved in with the bare minimum of belongings. Our furniture and other items will be delivered in a couple of weeks. We were on a tight schedule, so the girls would be settled and ready to start at their new schools. The girls loved the house and have their own rooms. The pool (which I did not want) was the best thing ever to them. After years of dreaming, I finally felt that I had made it. Owning a home was the final task I needed to accomplish to feel like I became everything my mother said that I couldn't.

It is the 2nd day of school. Lexi started 5th grade at the middle school, and Marie-Elena started kindergarten. Sammy is almost two years old and stays home with us. She has never seen a daycare. The big difference from the New Jersey schools is that kindergarten is a half-day program. Marie-Elena has to be picked up from school at 11:20. I am working at my desk. It is just after 10 am; when my cell phone rings. It is a local number, so I do not ignore the call. The woman on the line is the secretary from the elementary school. She proceeds to ask me if Marie-Elena is absent today. I was like, what do you mean she is absent? I put her on the bus that morning. The secretary goes I will call you back before I can get another word out, she hangs up on me. I am immediately in a panic. I am not dressed for going out, but I do not care. I find shoes yelling at Rob to get Sammy ready, that the school lost our child. We are almost in the car, prepared to make the four-mile drive to the school, when the school calls me again. The secretary informs me that two girls were absent from the kindergarten class that day, and by elimination, they figured out that my child was found wandering down the busy back road where the bus depot is.

We bundle up and get to the school. I am trying not to lose my mind on the principal and superintendent that they lost my child on the 2nd day of school. Instead, I focus on following Sammy, who is toddling up and down the sidewalk. Toddle, toddle, toddle, turn, and repeat. Following her moves making sure she does not fall or go into the school parking lot keeps me from breaking down. Rob is talking to the school staff while we wait for the officer and the woman who found my child to bring her back to the school. I catch some of the conversations with Rob and the school staff. He has always been better at keeping his cool than me, plus he is better with people, so I let him talk. Apparently, Marie-Elena fell asleep on the bus, and no one made sure she got off at the school. The bus driver then took the bus to the depot for the day. He never checked the bus at the school or the depot to make sure it was empty or clean. Marie-Elena eventually opened the bus door, and then she started walking up the road looking for a grown-up.

Luckily a travel nurse got lost on her way y to an appointment, letting her find Marie-Elena walking down the side of the road. We had only lived in town for about two weeks now, and she did not know her school name or address by heart yet. With calls, the police and schools figured out who she is and what school she should be at. The cop allows the nurse to follow him to the school with Marie-Elena in her car. I was grateful a five-year-old did not have to be alone in the back of a cop car. Having my five-year-old step out of a stranger's car running towards me, breaking down was too much. I always knew that I loved my kids and would die for them, but a part of me always worried I would be like Barbara, and when shit hit the fan, I would realize I was incapable of loving them the way they deserved. I was wrong. My kids have my heart. By the time I had my baby back, there was less than an hour of school left. We decided to take the kids to lunch and to shop for the afternoon. I needed the time away with them to regroup.

The next day we had Marie-Elena take the bus, and we followed behind for a couple of days to ensure she was okay. Rob and I agreed she had to face the fear of the bus because she had many more years of school to go. While things could have turned out so much worse, I am grateful that my child was brought back to me. I am very lucky things turned out the way they did. Unfortunately, other parents have not been so fortunate. The school fired the bus driver and, over the next couple of weeks, created protocols for checking the buses to ensure something like this would not happen again.

The holiday season of 2018 is upon us, and Tami and her husband, John, have come to visit for a night on their way to New York for a few days. It was beautiful to finally be able to have a home she could stay at and that I wanted to show off. But, as always, after a day of fun with Tami, the girls do not want her to leave.

The next couple of years fly by with no significant events, thankfully. Then, the pandemic hits, seemingly changing the whole world overnight. The kids hate virtual school and have a more challenging time with academics. I have worked at home for years, so I did not experience any changes in my work. We did see a drop in income as many doctors were not allowed in nursing homes or to do elective surgeries. The reduction in patient visits meant a decrease in billing, causing me a loss of money. However, I was still grateful to have a job when others were not so lucky.

Chapter 38

May 27th, 2020, Barbara is up for parole once again. With the pandemic, protocols changed with how hearings are held. Prior I always attended via a phone call. If I wanted to participate via teleconference, I would have had to go to a courthouse to be able to participate in the hearing with visuals. Now we are able to attend via zoom in our homes. I was having a new level of anxiety with being able to see Barbara after twenty years. The last time I saw her was at her sentencing when I was fifteen years old. When she appeared on screen, I felt fearful. Like seeing her would somehow make me inferior or incapable in some way. My first thought is that she looks so old. Her beauty was lost many years ago. Now, instead of a cute grandmother type, I see evil. I am glad

I do not have to speak until the end of the hearing. By then, I am able to get my shit together so I can speak against her release.

The process is the same they review her prison history and review her plan for release. Things have been the same for her no new trouble, and she is still the same religion. The hearing goes on, and she contradicts herself many times and, by the end, still cannot fully accept her part in my sister's murder. Tami and I spoke at the end, both of us hopeful that she will not be released. The hearing seemed faster, maybe because it was just a repeat of the same stories. In the end, she was denied for another three years. At the conclusion of the hearing, the D.A. called me to tell me he was shocked they denied her, California laws have changed, and she is deemed a low threat to the public. He advised me that unless there is something new or she starts getting violations in prison, it is highly likely that she will be released at her next hearing. I did not want to hear that, but I felt the same way.

Chapter 39

My health has always been a priority to me. I have eye issues that may have stemmed from the bleach in my eyes. When I was pregnant the first time, it was determined that I have a genetic kidney disease. Working out and eating well did not help. In the summer, I had my right kidney removed. Having the surgery completely changed my health for the better. While I still have to be careful and monitored, my recurrent infections have all but disappeared. The month following my surgery, Tami spent a few days with us. It was wonderful to show her the town I call home and do fun things with the girls. None of us wanted her to go back home.

I have always had trouble finding the need to fight to make a relationship work. I can move on knowing I will be just fine, easier than most people. I have not talked to my father in over 13 years. He never really wanted to grow up and be a father. I tried to have a relationship with him and a future where he was my kid's grandfather. He did not want to work that hard and took his wife's word for the truth. I am not asking for him to go against her, but I would have liked him to try at least to maintain a relationship with me. Hell, I moved across the country to get to know him. I do not regret the move at all.

I was unlucky that my parents should have never been parents. My relationship with my aunts and uncles fizzled out as well. I stopped reaching out, and then so did they. I wish I was better at fighting for what is essential in the way of family bonds. I wish my kids had more interactions with the living family I have left. I am so used to people leaving and family never meant forever. I would give up if things got too much. After giving up, I would be angry that my family did not fight more to have me in their lives. That has been my whole life, wanting a family that would love me and fights to stay by my side even when I am not at my best. I am blessed to have Rob and Tami, who have never given up on our relationships and stayed around even when I may not have deserved them too.

A few years back I became reacquainted with Holly and Mike via the wonderful world of Facebook. I was hopeful that they found happiness and were leading fulfilling lives. I will always have love for Holly and Mike. Mike was my first everything. I wanted so much for his future. I always thought it would be tied to mine. Unfortunately, that was not the case. While I am blessed in the life I have created, Holly and Mike do not have the same. Last I heard, they are both addicted to drugs. Mike is homeless, sometimes living with his mom in a tent at the river bottoms. His oldest child is lucky and has a great mother who cares for her well. His youngest was born drug-addicted and taken by child services. Holly has married the man she was with as a teenager. I believe they have four children, three girls, and a boy. They have lost all four of them. The last official update I had on Holly was in mid-2020. She was in the hospital for something and almost died, and she was pregnant at the time and lost the baby. It is so heartbreaking knowing how they are living and all the hours we talked about our futures. Sadly, they were not able to break the cycle, do the hard work and be better than they were raised. I am glad I broke off contact when I did. I could not live the way they have chosen. I wish them the best and hope they can find a way out of the hell they created for themselves. Sometimes it is just easier to become a statistic.

The year of changes 2022. Lexi is a freshman in high school, taking three honors classes and Spanish two. She has always been intelligent, quickly obtaining honor roll status each semester. Marie- Elena started fourth grade. While learning does not come as quickly to her, she is everyone's friend. I am so proud of the sweet girl that never singles anyone out and always befriends those that are bullied. Sammy Doodle (Samantha) started Kindergarten, and she loves making friends. I am sad that my baby is now in school. I am blessed to have them and love watching them grow, but I wish it would slow down just a little. I received a letter stating that Larry was up for his first attempt at parole. I was in the process of requesting to be a part of the hearing, but I was not sure whether I wanted him to be released or not. While Larry had his role in the abuse, I know Barbara was the mastermind behind it all. I also do not think Larry, now in his 70s, would try to find me. So I was not entirely against the idea of him being released. It turns out it did not matter what I thought; I received another letter stating that Larry voluntarily waived his right to a hearing for a year. I was dumbfounded that he would not even try to get paroled.

The year progressed, and in early September, I received a letter that Barbara is up for parole again, and her next hearing is to be held on December 7th. So, as I always do when I get a letter from the parole board I start searching the internet for any articles regarding the case. I do not know why I torture myself searing for information, but I just want to find a way to feel closer to Alexia. What gets to me the most is that no one remembers Alexia. Most of the people who knew her passed on. During this search, I found a book written by a former FBI agent. The book has been out for a few years, but I must have missed it in my past searches. The book was written by one of the FBI agents who interviewed me about my sister's disappearance/death. Chapter five is our case. I immediately bought the book, so grateful someone has cared enough about her short life to include her history in a book about his most notable cases. I reached out to Jeff via Facebook messenger to thank him for including Alexia and remembering her. Jeff and I eventually spoke on the phone and were able to clear the air. I was a teenager with a bad attitude when, he interviewed me, and he was to me a bully. I understand now it was an excellent tactic to get information, but back then, it just pissed me off. Jeff vowed to help me in any way he could to keep Barbara and Larry behind bars.

Getting closer to her parole hearing date caused me a tremendous amount of anxiety this time around. I have never been so anxious that it affected my work. My fear of her getting out was taking hold. I even had to add an anxiety medication to get my life back to normal. Knowing Barbara is getting older and that the parole board has different guidelines for those considered senior citizens. I thought for sure she would be released. All this extra emotional distress allowed me to finally realize that maybe it was time for me to seek therapy.

Chapter 40

I sat at my desk via video conference on December 7, 2022, while waiting for the hearing to start. I was so sure she would be released. Even the D.A. thought her chances were good. In truth, we need a miracle. The commissioner started the hearing. The panel will give special consideration to the elderly parole factors and decide your suitability for parole today. Once again, they go through her history in prison and acknowledge any new self-help courses she had taken since the last hearing. Barbara was asked if she was a danger to the community. Her response floored me. I was dangerous. Not so much in people outside my house, but to people in my house, yes, very much so. That makes it all better. She is not a risk to anyone outside her own home, so as long as she lives alone, it will all be okay. At that point, I was already annoyed that I could not speak until my turn to give a statement. She then tells the board the reason for her crimes is that she is/was angry. The anger she carried from her childhood abuse led her to lash out.

The panel asks questions, and she fumbles with her plan to avoid drugs and codependent relationships. The final statements are given, and Barbara does not even seem to try. It is concise, thanking the panel for their time. Barbara states she is not the same person she was then and that she is really sorry. I almost felt bad for the lack of convection in her statement. For the first part of the hearing, I thought for sure she was going to win. She was saying all of the right things, taking full responsibility for her actions, and even playing the remorse card well. I felt sick to my stomach. Then she floundered on the panel's questions and lacked a complete plan for release. I also had a bit of hope because I added Jeff, the FBI agent who worked the case as a victim representative, allowing him the right to speak against Barbara at the hearing. He was a surprise guest. No matter the outcome, I am grateful for his help and for keeping his word to help me.

Jeff's statement: "I am a retired special agent from the Federal Bureau of Investigation. I was one of the investigating, uh, officers for this matter. I have, uh, eyewitness and smell and visual memory, clear, vivid memory of the crime scene that when we entered after that home. I saw the picture with the face cut out. We took apart the fireplace in the home brick by brick and sent it to Virginia Laboratory, trying to find one organic molecule that would be from Alexia. We disinterred ten dogs. And opened them up, looking for the child's remains, and found none. I would like to submit to the panel that we served five search warrants on that home. And at one point, I was there at the home, and we received a phone call from, uh, Ms. Carrasco. I spoke with her on the telephone. She had been in jail for several, uh, days already. And when she spoke to me, she was not under the influence of drugs or anything else. And as a result, when I did speak to her, she once again told me that the child was with her natural father in Chicago, which of course, was not true. She then asked me to do things to assist her in covering up what she and Larry Carrasco had done. Whether she was aware she was speaking to the law enforcement person or not, I don't know, but it was clear to me that she was continuing in her effort to hide the crime. I am here today to support Jessica, and I would like to say that after the bleach was poured on Jessica, she was removed to the child's receiving home. I am the FBI agent that went there and interviewed her. And the interview with Jessica turned into an emotional breakdown by Jessica, which I've been waiting 25 years to apologize to her for. It was Jessica that provided the information that enabled us to determine what happened in this scenario. Jessica contacted me four months ago after, uh, which was the first time I heard, had heard from her. I had been searching for her for 25 years to apologize for what she had to go through to account for what had happened. I want the panel to know what caused Jessica's emotional breakdown, and the revelation of what happened was going over the entire period where she was actually the mother, the defender, and the protector. She attempted to keep Alexia alive, and she failed. And she's lived her whole life knowing that she's failed. I lived my whole life smelling the ten dogs, wanting them to be opened in search of a child's remains, and being at the Sacramento River, where divers were put at risk because of the conditions. And I wonder how do you mitigate that if you let her out on parole? So, when we're discussing this crime, this crime occurred. I find it hard to believe that Ms. Carrasco cannot remember many of the things she participated in. I was one of the arresting officers when she was provided with the arrest warrant in jail. And when she was provided with the arrest warrant in jail, she immediately confessed and blamed it on Larry. I believe that Ms. Carrasco minimizes and tries to avoid responsibility, but most importantly, what is important to me as a person who's worked this crime and been involved with it and seen the heinousness of it is Jessica, how can we, in society, possibly justify letting this person out in society where she can contact her daughter or just the knowledge that she's free and the anxiety, the fear that it would cause for her would re-victimize her. How can we justify re-victimizing one of the most horrendous crimes I've ever seen? I have a, I have a lot of notoriety for my success, my ability to be, to solve cases. I have never in my career. I've never in my life experienced a case where the offenders so thoroughly and completely removed another person's identity from life. Removed her. Recently I received a picture from Jessica, one of the last pictures taken before Alexia was killed. One picture, when Jessica contacted me, she thanked me for remembering Alexia because until then, she was the only one. How can we as a society allow a person among us who has not only done this to a six-year-old child but, let's not forget the 13-year-old sister that was tortured as well, forced to drink bleach. She survived because she had the facilities and mental stability to survive. She tried to save her sister but was not able to and was forced to watch her sister die and forced to see what was done with her body. I'm here representing Jessica because there is no way in my life I could sit by and allow the possibility of Ms. Carrasco being released, knowing what trauma that would cause in Jessica's life."

My statement followed: Every time we have another hearing, it is closer and closer to her being released just because she's old and maybe ill. Okay, that's fine and dandy. I'm getting older, and I have ailments too. You don't see me using that as an excuse for beating and killing my children. I have three children. I get angry every day. I have a 13-year-old who talks back and wants to live on her phone but not doing chores. I'm angry. Do I beat her? Do I lock her in her room, have her windows nailed shut, and not let her out? Do I force her to drink bleach by myself?

No, I don't do any of those things because I know I brought those children into this world whether I wanted them at the time or not. It's still my responsibility to care for them, and if I didn't want them or the responsibility, I should have given them up for adoption. You did not want us. Thank you. I need that. Thank you for finally telling the truth, Barbara, that you didn't want us. I knew that, but you kept us around because we were beneficial to you for whatever reason. You are sitting in there, and I'm out here still terrified that you're going to get out, come in my door, and I'm going to be my 12- year old self all over again and not be able to fight back.

I will not do that to myself. I won't do that to my children. But I'm angry. I have mental health problems. I have not gone to drugs. I've gone to a therapist, I've gone to a doctor, I worked out, I do things that are beneficial for me, and I do things because you always said I couldn't. Telling me I'd be pregnant at 13 and wouldn't graduate high school. Obviously, I did all those things; I am none of those things. I, I have a bachelor's degree. I have my own business. I have three healthy, beautiful daughters. I have my own home and vehicles—all of those things. And I did it all in spite of you and in spite of what you did. This is not right where you're living, not my five-year-old sister. She had never got to go to kindergarten, never had to got to get friends, go to her birthday party. I've been doing all of these things with my children. My six-year-old started kindergarten. She has friends and a birthday party with her friends. All of these things, unless you could give her back and let her have those things, and my family have her. You don't deserve to be out, whether you're old or sick.

The board came back with their decision. Based on the legal statements and the evidence considered, we find that you do pose an unreasonable risk to public safety and are, therefore, not suitable for parole. Today, we also gave special consideration to your advanced age, length of incarceration, and your diminished physical condition. Specifically, we determine these factors may somewhat reduce your risk for future violence. Today, you are 60 years old, you have been in CDCR custody for 22 years. Physically, you do have some mobility issues, and you use the walker, but you still may possess an ability to perpetrate some acts of violence though your mobility limitations may mitigate your risk to some extent. Cognitively the panel did not see any age-related decline. Today, we found the factors mitigate your current risk that were outweighed by factors to aggravate your current risk.

The first is being yourself control. We did see in your crime you were unable to control your behavior as a result of one and more of the following, you were callous toward others. We saw that you were too deep into your addiction to think about what you were doing in poisoning and killing your daughter. And you didn't consider the pain that she was in or the memory or the trauma you were putting your other daughter through. We also saw that you had a criminal attitude. It did appear that you were more concerned with getting out than your surviving daughter's well—being. And you put her through an unspeakable crime by forcing her to witness the mutilation of her dead's sister's body and to assist in disposing of it. Today, we didn't find your offender change to be aggravating, and despite programming, you do continue to express views that demonstrate a lack of change. You continue to lack self-awareness of the causative factors of your crime. You haven't figured out why you did what you did. You are more likely to do it or something similar again as you don't know what to watch out for to prevent yourself from being involved in similar behaviors in the future. Therefore, we find there's clear and convincing evidence that neither a 10 nor a 15-year denial is appropriate in consideration of victim public safety. Instead, your next scheduled parole suitability hearing shall be set in three years' time.

I was relieved I was getting another three-year denial. This could mean only two years, as Barbara can request an earlier hearing if she is well-behaved. When I had spoken at prior hearings, I would be redirected not to address Barbara directly. During this hearing, the board did not correct me. I wonder why. I am glad they allowed it. Speaking more directly to Barbra gave me a greater sense of power. Speaking directly to her made me feel empowered and less cowardly. I only wish she would have had bad behavior while incarcerated. If she did, the board could make the denial term longer. I do not think I will ever fully understand how she can be so behaved and stay away from drugs while incarcerated but never could before. Barbara states she has been sober since the day of her arrest, 10-1-1997. We all know any prisoner could have access to drugs if they wanted. Why did she make a choice to stay clean now? Why did she have to ruin so many lives with her own selfish ways? The person she is now is the person I wish I could have known. Now no matter who she becomes, her image to me will always be that of the evil, hateful drug addict who had no love for the children that should have been her world. Will I ever be able to understand my life and her role in it when

25 years later, she is still not being truthful? It is tough to

find my truth when my present is still full of past lies.

Chapter 41

With the success of the most recent parole hearing, I was still determined to start trauma therapy. I had way more stress and anxiety prior to this hearing than ever before. Something inside was changing, and I could not handle it. All areas of my life were suffering. The two primary goals I had when considering therapy were to help me be a better parent and to learn how to handle myself and my emotions if Barbara gets released. I had found myself many times over the years sounding a lot like Barbara when I lost my cool. The words and my tone hurt my heart. I needed to act; I cannot let Barbara control my life in any way. At one point, I thought if the hearing went my way, I would be okay, but I soon realized that I needed to finally process the horrors I lived through. EMDR therapy is no joke. I felt like I was reliving the most horrific moments of my life again. I was not sure I would go back after that first session. But, I went back and will continue to do so until I can find a way to be at peace with my past.

A few weeks into therapy I have had some breakthroughs and changes in my thinking patterns. My initial thought, when asked about my past, is that I was a coward, I did not do enough to change our situation and was not able to save my sisters life. For the last 25 years, I have beaten myself up for not seeking help. Before my sister's murder, I had never considered what my parents were doing as abuse. To me, abuse would leave marks and be physically painful. The idea of verbal or emotional abuse was too abstract. The week before Alexia's death was when most of the physical abuse occurred, and by that point, it was summer, and I was locked up in a bedroom for more hours than I was not. I honestly had no access to get help for us. Barbara spent years trying to break me. Alexia's death showed me what they were truly capable of. I knew without a doubt they could kill me. During those times of complete isolation, I often wished for death. I wanted all of the pain I was feeling to end. It is exceedingly difficult to process pain when you do not understand why things are happening. Do I have regrets and a ton of survivor's guilt? Yes, I do, and I think I will still have them, no matter how much therapy or time that goes by. I want them to stop holding back my emotional growth and connections with people. Emotional development is one of the hardest things for me personally to address. As a child living with Barbara, she took away all of my choices,

I had no power. I did not know any different. It was years of programming by Barbara to make me the victim she wanted. Making her kids feel like nothing made her feel like something. I always wanted my mother's love, and until it all became real, and her threats were no longer threats, I knew I would never get the mother I wanted or deserved. For years after the event, part of me still wanted my mom to love me. Now 25 years later, I know that is never going to happen. She has only and will forever only love herself. After having my own children and knowing what a mother's love feels like and what I want my children to feel, I came to terms with not being blessed with a mother's love and affection. I know I missed out on something truly life-changing. It is sad but also okay. The events of my life have brought me to a place I never thought deep down that I deserved. I think the only thing I would change in my past is my sister's death.

I would still go through the rest of the abuse, foster care, and surviving on my own to become the person I am today. I learned so many things the hard way. Most of my drive to succeed was to be everything my mother said I couldn't be and to do all the things my sister could not. Living in the shadow of someone who is a memory has been difficult. I have accepted that while my motivations were always geared towards spiting Barbara or living because Alexia cannot, the goals I reached and the success I achieved were still done by my hard work. I have learned that I can be proud of who I am and what I have become, even if I am not always doing it for myself. Letting go of the guilt piece by piece is giving me the freedom I have always craved.

I spend time thinking of why Barbara is the way she is, hoping that in each of these parole hearings, I will learn something that makes any of the past make sense. It never comes. I need to let go of wanting an answer because the answer is one I never wanted to hear. She never loved or wanted her children. We were always in the way and useless she could use us to benefit her in some way. We were useless. Hearing your mother admit she never wanted you or loved you and wanted you dead is unthinkable. I heard that in the last hearing, and it set me free. I am thankful she finally admitted what I knew all along. Now I do not feel guilty about how if feel about her.

There is no part of me that sees her as my mother any longer. The validation of what I had felt for years was calming to my twisted, tortured soul. Barbara seems to have at least made some changes to better herself over the years and is now a mentor/mom to the new lifers that come into the prison. I do not want to call Barbara mom, but I do not want anyone else to either. That is not a title she will ever deserve. I am also finding more anger towards her, I thought I put it behind me long ago, but getting past my feeling of being a failure, I have found anger. I am pissed that other inmates are getting mothering from the person who should have given it to me. There is a fleeting thought that what was so wrong with me that my mother did not love or want me but can so easily do for other women now. I am angry that her decisions not only affected me when they happened but are still influencing my life now. I wonder what my life could have been if I did not have to go through foster care or had a family to fall back on as a young adult. I would have had other choices. It does not matter now because I found my version of happy in the end. My dreams changed and I changed, but it was not all bad. With hard work and determination, I broke the cycle of abuse. I am proud that I did not become a statistic. Many times, over the years just giving up and doing drugs or stopping my education was the easier choice. I often wanted to take drugs or drink in my bouts of loneliness and depression. I am eternally grateful I was able to stay strong and become a person I can be proud of. Hopefully, Alexia is proud too.

In sharing, I hope to help even one person know their worth and fight for the life they want, no matter their past. Strength comes from within. Tap into it and be your best you despite hard times or the evil people in our lives. I was dealt a horrible hand in life, but I survived. I am no longer a victim. I am a survivor. I am not broken.

Chapter 42

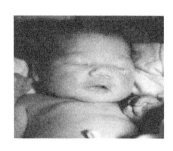 

Alexia Ann September 23, 1997   *Alexia's 1ˢᵗ Birthday*

Alexia, Chad, and I

Alexia and I Christmas 1996

Alexia age 5   Alexia and Granny

Last Photo May 1997

Granny and I. Last Christmas Together (2000)

News Article photo of Larry and Barbara.

November 1997

Printed in Great Britain
by Amazon

25249319R00175